WILDFLOWER

Reclaiming a Sacred Place

ZOE ANA BELL
Sydney, Australia

Copyright © 2021 Zoe-Anna
Wildflower- Reclaiming A Sacred Place

Uterus 6 Art by Emma Plunkett – Licence for rights to use. Book cover design: Mala Letra Diseño Editorial.

All rights reserved. No part of this book may be used or reproduced by any means, graphic, electronic, or mechanical including photocopying, recording, taping or by any information storage retrieval system without the written permission of the author except in the case of brief quotations embodied in critical articles and reviews.

The information, ideas, and suggestions in this book are not intended as a substitute for professional medical advice. Before following any suggestions contained in this book, you should consult your personal physician. Neither the author nor the publisher shall be liable or responsible for any loss or damage allegedly arising as a consequence of your use or application of any information or suggestions in this book.

Because of the dynamic nature of the Internet, any web addresses or links contained in this book may have changed since the publication and may no longer be valid. The views expressed in this work are solely those of the author and do not necessarily reflect the views of the publisher, and the publisher hereby disclaims any responsibility for them.

The author of this book does not dispense medical advice or prescribe the use of any technique as a form of treatment for physical, emotional, or medical problems without the advice of a physician, either directly or indirectly. The intent of the author is only to offer information of a general nature to help you in our quest for emotional and spiritual well-being. In the event you use any information in this book for yourself, which is your constitutional right, the author and the publisher assume no responsibility for your actions.

Wildflower – Reclaiming A Sacred Place - Ms. Zoe Anna Bell
Book 2 of the trilogy series: FREE WILDFLOWER CODES
Publication 21st December, 2021 RAW Publishing
ISBN: 978-0-6481776-4-7

Dedication

This book is dedicated to You the reader. At the time when I began writing my story, it was a journey to finding myself. A path of Soul remembrance as I began to unravel the layers and explore the womb mysteries and how to reclaim my Feminine divinity. A perfect path of experiences to be a guide for women, men and youth. I am a pioneer who dared to walk her own path and expose what was ready to reveal all to create space for deep inner healing and transformation.

This is for all of you that have been shamed, judged, felt guilty and who blame their bodies in some shape or form. This is dedicated to celebrating feminine sensual wholeness and to shift beyond sexual objectivity of lustful desires. It is time to forgive your forgetfulness and remember how to heal your innocence, no matter your biology or ideology.

No matter your biology or ideology, you came here to experience and express being human. You each came to Earth to learn and grow through diverse life experiences. A path to learning to love you and set your Spirit free.

As a child you used your senses to explore the world in play and curiosity. Natural play is now being placed into a box by wounded adults, all to create gender confusion. For example, a four-year-old girl seen playing with trucks and then defined as being orientated as transgender. This gender confusion is driven by unhealed and traumatised adults with a sick agenda playing out. And it is being sold to those vulnerable and living in a state of fear. Welcome to an aspect of the depopulation plan.

Breastfeeding is being replaced with chest feeding and birthing mothers are replaced with the term *'birthing person'*. Not only is the Vulva digitally castrated for magazines, but horrific practices of Female Genital Mutilation are also still happening around the world. Women's rights and the rites of sacred passage into womanhood is getting blended and eliminated by a sick minority of the cancel culture. Women are designed to nourish pregnancies within her natural womb if she chooses and we have two sexes, male and female. The mRNA vaccination for a so-called plan-demic is impacting the sacred womb and future fertility, another ploy of depopulation and de-humanisation.

This is dedicated to all who have a charge and objection around talking about sensuality and even the words Vulva, Pussy and Cunt. I invite you into deeper insights into how your fears create limitations and how wrong thinking creates body restrictions, disease, and sexual disempowerment. It is my intention to guide you to freedom with reflective reverence and sensual empowerment.

It is time to celebrate the fact that many of you entered the world, through your Mums open, extremely wise, engorged and expanded pinkish mauve vagina. Some of you may have entered the world through a C-section. Most of you were made as a result of sex, and some may have been made in a test-tube, then artificially inseminated. All will have grown in a magical dark place, called the womb. Women are Divine in design created by Source/God, as are men in his own Divine biology. As a society let's not give up the Rites of Passage of Women and the Rites of Passage of Men and remember the sacredness of sensuality. Do this for your children if nothing else as these rights are getting take away to feed a nefarious agenda that is playing out. Scribed, June 2021.

Biology is biology and ideology a choice and not for others to accept you. True acceptance is learning to love yourself from the inside out beyond external validation. If you are Transgender, then before you throw your wig or lipstick at me, this book is for You. I've worked with many transgender blends in the past and honestly, they don't carry on like the media portrays. I see love in all beings as your genitals do not define you and no one cares about your sexual exploration and there is no logical reason why your sexual orientation has to be such a big focus on your job. You are there to share your gifts as a co-creator in your service contribution and unless sex is a part of your job then it has zero relevance!

It is your natural sensual essence that connects you to all that is, and this is your life force. The truth is the more surgery you have, the more scar tissue you create and the harder it is for your Spirit to breathe in the meat body suit. This is dedicated to all that are numb, disconnected and drowning on the inside, perhaps suffocating in their skin, shame and sin.

I've dedicated this trilogy to include teenagers who feel hijacked by comparison from the glossy magazines and the naive opinion of teenage boys that have innocently compared a natural Vagina/Vulva to that of an air-brushed and digitally touched up version found in a porn magazine and porn movies. It is time to tease this topic wide open. There is collective healing ready to be addressed, opened and innocence restored! If this makes you uncomfortable as a parent, then it is time to look at your own shame and unhealed traumas to break the chain of transference along generations.

This book takes you on a journey of self-acceptance, unapologetic self-love and a delightful doorway to deepen intimacy of self being an awakened woman. Aspects to be integrated for when you choose to be intimate with another. This book is infused with life experiences as a path of initiation to activate remembrance. To be where I am now. It is time to be shameless and unfuckwithable.

It is my intention to bring lightness into the darkness to invite humour as we dance along this adventure side by side. It is your human right to have freedom to choose with who to explore your body and also your sexual preferences.

Sensuality is your human birth right and it's been clouded by manipulation of sex, dirtied up, controlled by the media, perverts all with a twisted sick agenda that want you to stay small, insignificant and obedient. It is time for many adults to grow up into adulthood and begin the journey to truly honouring the feminine vessel and not see her as a birthing machine, object of sexual desire or a pleasure center to lift you up. SHE is way more than that and the wise women are rising as the courageous leaders of the New Earth.

Contents

FOUR WORDS XVII

INTRODUCTION 1

CHAPTER 1: DIVINE SOURCE GODDESS 9
Do you love what you see? 9
What clouds perception? 11
Different name for the female genitalia? 17
The Three Faces of the Goddess 22
    APHRODITE The Free Maiden 22
    GAIA- The Earth Mother 23
    ISIS: Return of the Queen 25
The development task of the Crone 26

CHAPTER 2: THE DESIGNER VAGINA 33
Yoni Healing 33
Facing a fear wide open 35
Removing Healthy Tissue 38
What is Labiaplasty? 41

The Barbie Doll Vagina 42
A cultural contrast 45
Positive Awareness in the Media 46

CHAPTER 3: HIJACKED BY COMPARISON 51

Comparison Hostage 51
Yoni feedback from the Men and Women 54
Aesthetics over performance 59
Body confidence 60

CHAPTER 4: RAW FEMININE POWER 69

The Power of Presence 69
Self-confidence - inner radiance 74

CHAPTER 5: TOUCH FOR HUMAN SURVIVAL 81

Touch and Development 81
The Benefits of Touch 86
    Physical level: 86
    Endorphins are released = Happiness 86
    Emotional level: 87
    letting go and receiving love. 87
    Psychological level: 87
    It feels good & soothing. 87
    Spiritual level: 88

Touch reaches deep into the Soul......................................88

  Shifting from Numbness to Sensation 89

Exploring Masturbation 91

CHAPTER 6: HEALTHY SENSUALITY & HEALING RITUALS ...93

Sexuality and Sensuality 93

Breathing and trusting in letting go 96

what are you holding onto? 98

The N.S Arousal Response in the Body............................100

Breathing Awareness Rituals...101

  You-niverse Breath..101

  Mirror Work - I Love You 103

  Body Love Through Movement................................106

Body work for Yoni Healing..108

  Yoni-verse Breath..108

  Flowering Lotus..111

  Yoni Love Flowering Ritual......................................112

  Deeper Healing 114

  A Potent Jewel within 116

A Correlation Between the Throat and Yoni 116

  Open up and Moan 117

  For the Women 118

  For the Men 119

Intimacy Rituals in Coupling 120
    Cosmic breath with your Beloved 120
    Playful and Healthy Sensation Exploration 122

CHAPTER 7: A FLOWERING YONI 123

The Womb- a sacred place 123

Reclaiming Your Womb 126
    Clearing Old Contracts 127

The Blood Mysteries 128
    Moon Practices 130

CHAPTER 8: AWAKENING & CONSCIOUS RELATIONSHIPS . 135

Expanding sensuality 135
    growing into adulthood 138
    Behind The Scenes 139

What is Spiritual Connection? 143
    What is blocking spiritual connection? 145

A Conscious Divine Union 146
    Co-Creating a Symbiotic Relationship 148
    Co-Existing in Relationship 150
    Open Relationships 152
    Dishonouring Lifeforce 156
    Non- Monogamy 158

CHAPTER 9: EXPRESSING INTIMATE DESIRES 167

Choosing your Vibe 167

    different states on the energy resonance scale. 169

Up level your Relationship 171

    Express Raw Vulnerability... 171

    Deepen Intimacy 172

    Create Trust 173

    Set Boundaries 174

    Know your Boundaries 174

    Open Communication... 177

    Be in Non-judgment.. 177

CONCLUSION 183

A Woman of Ease & Grace 189

BIBLIOGRAPHICAL RESOURCES................................... 193

ACKNOWLEDGMENTS 195

ABOUT THE AUTHOR 197

SALES PAGE 199

Four words

Simplicity and space are keys to freedom. The wisdom of the womb is rich in creative natural flowing order. I pondered this aspect of the book with innocent curiosity as I received the sacred words that flowed from 22 men and women. Here are 11 with the other 11 added into *Breaking Free – No More Soul Suffocation*.

The question was.

'Can you give me a Synopsis of Zoe in 4 words.'

Georgina Playstead: Bodacious – Courageous – Ninja Warrior

Norman Sparrow: Wild – Unapologetic – Eccentric – Bold

Tania Wursig: Maverick – Unapologetic – Open – Compassionate

Donald Shakes: Solidarity – Love – Humble – Inner Strength

Tammy de Roncox: Boldness – Spirited – Devotional – Ineffable

Brett Manning: Beautiful Soul – Pleiadean Priestess

Sarah Ployakov: Interdimensional – Embodied – Cosmic Creator

Shaz Sass: Powerful – Sexy – Raw – Real

Deb Beacroft: Magic – Powerful – Sacred Goddess/Wombman – Courageous

Stevie Levine: Fluid – Lucid – Open - Connected

Seanchai Séance: Powerful – Innovative – Creative – Nurturing

11:11 in Honour to one of my Teachers, Chief Standing Elk passed over in July 2021. His Spirit is infinite and honouring all the work he has done for humanity and standing for peace, love, harmony, freedom and UNITY for all beings.

11:11 holds much symbology which is shared in *Soul Codes – Remembering your Mission.*

And so it is

And so it was

And so it shall be….

Forever Free.

Introduction

There is nothing more vulnerable than talking about your most vulnerable and sacred place, yes? Women's genitalia that have been over-sexualised, misused and fed off for way too long. It is my intention to infuse humour into topics that many in society still feel shame about, all to support healing and learning how to grow into your skin. If we cannot laugh and be light about life and have fun, then how will you ever reclaim pure innocence and joy?

Let's talk female genitalia. In the medical world the term Vagina is used, yet this is only the inner tube aspect and disregards the sacred, sensitive and powerful arousal tissues. The term Yoni or wildflower will be used as this encompasses everything, vagina, vulva, clitoris, clitoral shaft and womb. It is time to break the ice on a genitalia term that sends some into rage and some into lustful desire. To understand it's true meaning, the true origin of this culturally offensive term will have to be disclosed as it is another form of mind manipulation and feminine disempowerment.

More so than right now, it is pivotal to dissolve the ways you have judged Self or others when it comes to the body, genitals and heal the wounds from within. Society is becoming more fake, distorted and full of 'over-sensitive' judgmental humans. The wounded inner child playing out as the entitled righteous ego, that has not done the inner work and expecting others to pander all to stop them feeling uncomfortable. Fuck that, you have to be willing to get uncomfortable and see the shadows of you that are blocking the TRUTH.

In the original book, *The Adventures of Pink Fairway*, it was a journey of shifting from internal torment of shame, self-loathing and disgust towards my body to *Breaking Free*. This then became my memoir that you have just read, *Breaking Free*. A path of inner suffering and pain would be the perfect training ground for learning to how to love myself unconditionally and have acceptance for my blossoming wildflower. As I ventured upon the path of self-realisation, I began see the blessing of this sacred gift and the wisdom that would emerge through growing into my flesh. A journey to Soul remembrance as a Star seed into a star blossom. This was a message given to me from my guardian angels:

"Zoe-Anna, humanity was crying out, so you were birthed on a prayer. They may not want this, and yet, they need this. Never forget this on your journey, as they will throw stones and lash out in judgment. Now dear soul is your journey beginning to make sense?"

Here I am and yes.

This is a book to ignite your creative juices and activate your roaring lioness fierceness to stand for your Sovereign Rites as a woman and man. I stand in full radiance of beauty, as an empty vessel penetrated by a deep resonance of soul-orgasmic waves of love that intend to touch you across the ether. This is an invitation to become curious and explore the depths of your raw sacred heart. There is an invisible wave and golden thread where simultaneously across the globe fellow Soul Sisters and Soul Brothers are standing in raw feminine magnetism and connecting together to jump start the Earth beyond the 3rd dimensional Matrix where many are held bound in heavy density of mind programming. The uniting of men and women is part of a greater Soul mission to share these inspirational insights, expressed in writing, teachings, and being a voice of many sharing this ancient wisdom. Wise words from a friend and fellow light streaker of truth, Lee Parore.

INTRODUCTION

'Time to purge, this is the end to an era of domination. Our soul mission is to be in-harmony with self and that within'. Lee Parore

The intention of this book is to inspire another perspective (as nothing ancient can be new!) upon something magical, mystical and beautiful. Sadly, many in society experience shame and sin, hiding these emotions in the dark. Souls hijacked by comparison, thinking there is something wrong with them, 'down there', with a background of 'seething rage and shame'. If you are hearing phrases like, 'new age, new world order and new normal', then this is part of the clever agenda all to hook you into the illusion. It is time to dissolve the illusion we have been fed and re-claim the invisible feminine Goddess Source power. This is your inner power and a path to your infinite Spirit.

This is to inspire everyone to love every inch of their magical bodies and never allow themselves to think there is something wrong with their uniqueness, as every design is pure beauty. You are divine and it is vital to stand with ruthless responsibility, badass no hiding ownership and to know right from wrong. Do good in your actions that brings no harm to others with the information that you have at your fingertips at the time. Discern what is true and never give up your sovereignty. To compare yourself to a touched-up magazine is unrealistic and unhealthy to the human psyche and feeds low self-esteem and shame.

The celebration of Sacred Sensuality is the doorway to understanding your life-force energy and unveil the divinity as a Soul. Yes, healthy, juicy pink or purple or mauve labial flesh is being destroyed by digital castration for magazines while a large package on a man is celebrated and emphasised.

Every woman's body is divine with every size, shape and SHE is a work of art.

I've heard women asking, what is all the fuss about? Perhaps this book is for You, so you can explore what you've never been made aware of by having this wisdom passed on by the wise women in your family. Many women are brainwashed and cannot see as they are consuming so much T.V and the news, that their pineal gland has dried and shriveled up, and perhaps their vulvas that came here to be free are not being massaged and touched, due to shame and lost inner fire as they have rolled over into submission.

It is time to raise the bar by the way you act as loving guides for your children. To treat Mother Earth as she deserves as Mother Gaia is the sacred source feminine. To honour her with loving respect, and nourishing attention as this has a direct impact on the feminine essence of all humanity. Lands are being stripped, soils drained of nutrients, overused with the introduction of artificial pesticides and genetically modified organisms, all of which leech the soils natural fertility. The biological feminine is under the same onslaught with bodies pumped with artificial crap, toxins in your make-up, the mRNA jab, food and drinking water. The daily slaughter of toxicity from the paparazzi feeds the fear and low self-esteem catching a glimpse of the rich and famous make-up free, it is all a ploy of the agenda. People have no space to simply be, without the masks to think they look beautiful and psychological warfare is splashed all across the media outlets and if you buy these trashy magazines, then you are a part of the problem. I love to create with make-up, and I have also learnt to be unafraid to be seen and love the naked me. Fear, insecurity and doubt are inside jobs which you have to do the inner work as right now your insecurities are being fueled by the media controlling your mind and a

INTRODUCTION

thought process in self-destruct. The limiting belief of, 'I'm not good enough bullshit'.

Begin to embrace make-up-free time with the willingness to be seen and accept your natural glowing essence and notice how much you judge other women. It is freedom to be shameless and unapologetic to sit in a sacred circle with other women and open our legs where we all get to be seen by one another in the highest and deepest respect and unconditional love. There is something powerfully healing that happens in the presence of women supporting women and the power of the vulva which is getting silenced. This is the time of women rising and being heard and their wisdom listened to your vulva and throat are interconnected, once aligned potent presence is felt. We will not be silenced.

This path, I know many will throw stones of shame and my training ground set me up for what is ahead. I love my space, walking as the lone wolf and recognizing other powerful warriors which are the divine mirrors. I own my presence and retreat into my inner sanctum of nature as and when I choose. This is vital on the path of making a stand for something greater than body-image as many think we should just get over it or accept 'the new normal!' There it is again, the new world agenda getting sucked up and regurgitated by the sheeple and the so-called influencers that are assisting the agenda, all for recognition and success. Make it your mission to understand and inner-stand how to balance the powerful forces of nature, self-sanity and 'me-time' nourishment.

This has been and continues to be vital as I walk my Goddess warrior path and I am inviting you all along with me. Society may reject you and this is a gift ready to explore as it takes you into the wilderness of the darkest aspects. This is the real healing to learn how to never reject your Soul and set your Spirit free.

Everything in life is choice and free will. Each free will choice will have a consequence so make every choice a right choice with a clear conscience. Take time out for you as no one else will do it for you and stop apologising for being you to keep others comfortable.

This is true for when you read this book, when you need to put it down and step away, then do it. Listen to your body and soul as there is potency within stillness and silence. Your emotions are your spirit communicating to you to explore within.

Space is required for insights, to implement healthy practices of integration and allow the body to readjust and digest the content. Integration that is consistent develops improved pathways of love. It is not something that happens overnight. Included here are years of exploring, inner healing and trusting intuitive wisdom to lead me deeper into this work. Much more is passed on one to one where tender guidance and support is required beyond a book or digital series can do justice. I also wish to honour the sacredness of the feminine wisdom passed on in private sessions.

Shifting from awareness to integration is a path that takes weeks, months, and even years. Integration begins to evoke creative expression to flow with a deep connection to creativity and the sacral area. This stirring of creativity and birthing of fresh ideas overflows into the rising of the feminine in full embodiment. The final phase, re-birthing, and rising from the ashes again and again, as the divine emergence of You! This is a process to be navigated with gentleness and loving kindness.

This may not resonate with everyone, and that is a fact of life. I was never everyone's cup of tea and much of my life I was rejected or asked why I went the opposite way to others. Remember not to care what others think, and to keep coming back to the powerful and creative You.

INTRODUCTION

Initiation is navigated in the wilderness of the dark as the forward path is choosing to never look back and it is vital to step away from the pack and explore life as this is how you develop your wings. The wings at the back of your heart as an angel of light and the wings between your thighs, protecting your sacred chalice.

Embrace your Sacred Wildflower

Infinite gratitude, bliss and unconditional love,

Your healing guide, ally and See-Star

It is time for Star blossoming

Chapter 1: Divine Source Goddess

> *"I am divine magic, an infinite Source power, I am here to laugh, love and dance. I am here to align with my Soul purpose and celebrate life and contribute to humanity. I am a fearless Goddess, and I am free to be me."* – Zoe-Anna

Do You Love What You See?

Has your perception of what you see become blind and distorted?

This is the million-dollar question, and the majority of humans are not loving what they see, beating themselves up on a daily basis. Here is a suggestion, next time you walk past the mirror, shake your ass, stop, smile and say:

'Hey Gurl, you gorgeous goddess, check out your beauty and Sass!'

Put this book down and go do it. I want you to shine, and the time is now. You are here to own your full goddess essence and celebrate the inner sexy without holding anything back. Waiting for another to do it for you will bring you more pain, suffering, dressed up as disappointment. Play the game of life fearlessly and shamelessly with everything you are.

Is it NOW time to shift and change perspectives?

Ask if that what you see in the media has been used to brainwash your innocence? Not only by the media, the fashion industry and in 2020 and 2021, the social police on social media. The greatest enemy of all, hides within and most in society are expecting the world to change around them so they feel loved and accepted. Welcome to the back to front inverted nefarious game of de-humanisation. It is the inner critic that runs rampage in your mind, and this is the core and root cause of you that requires addressing.

The healing of the inner child and to change your thoughts by right-thinking and rewiring the mind to shift beyond the reptilian brain of fight and flight reactions. You cannot change the past and yet you can change your perspective and the meaning you give an event. Until you wake the fuck up and begin to see the clever games that keep you trapped, you will remain in a self-perpetuated prison of obedience and social performance. When you rise up and step out of line as the lone wolf, the many obedient sheeple will attempt to bring you down as it is the victim consciousness of humanity. It threatens their denial and refusal to look at the truth. Truth is the only reality.

Say hello to my little friend, the Tall Poppy syndrome!

(Imagine Al Pacino saying in the movie, Scarface)

This is some crazy-shit thing that Australian's love. Don't shine too bright, act too big and lordly forbid being too confident! To walk the path least travelled requires caring less and less what naysayers think! Let them talk. Be the inspiration for those that are afraid to shine bright and together let's stand out. It is your birth right and some are behind you for a reason. In saying that, many are watching in curiosity as they begin to step away from the hive mind of control.

Awaken Your flowering inner Sass!

WHAT CLOUDS PERCEPTION?

It is the mind that allocates meaning to what it sees and hence perceives. To shift beyond what is categorised by past experiences and have a logical thinking mind supported by inner knowing (intuition). This is key to expand a limited 'over-thinking' mind into limitless possibilities. Both sides of the brain have to work together as you have both sides for a reason. Inner wisdom and awareness are often hidden, shadowed by fear and reactivity of the reptilian brain. The individual learns to play games of manipulation to avoid judgement and disapproval and will avoid facing their fears and neurosis of wrong thinking. The bondage of the socialised mind of the Matrix and not having the courage to Neo-think.

To access inner wisdom requires turning the attention inwards with a calm and relaxed mind to remember what has been forgotten and dulled into suppression. You each have an ability to see into what is true and see through what we are being shown as the illusion of the game. To see where you are playing the game or getting played by others in the matrix. I repeat, learn to play the game beyond the game, or get played! You can stay in the washing machine of messing-up your life, feeling like you are being smashed by a tidal wave of internal self-destruct, or you can brave a path least ventured and be the change. The only way out, is in.

Embrace you and celebrate a body beautiful attitude to magnify your badass altitude. Unveil the passionate and classy woman from within. Ignite the inner vixen, energetic, bold, vibrant and free wild woman. Unleash you bad and nasty side in the bedroom as you are all of it. Those that are attracted to you, when they hear you speak of what you hate, detest or dislike about your body their sexual passion is killed.

It is one of the biggest turn-offs for a man.

If you wish to be desired, stop it **NOW!**

DIVINE SOURCE GODDESS

A man or woman loves and adores you for you, through their own eyes and heart. Stop messing up their beautiful magical picture with destructive nonsense of your inner critic. Take it from a woman who understands the minds and desires of men. Hearing bitching and complaining about others is a bore and a massive turn off. Guys hate it unless they are a bitch that loves to complain about life. Even worse is the toxicity it produces within the body affecting those around you that get to bathe in its *off-ness*. To witness another bitching and complaining about themselves is sad. For years I put my body down and this is a toxic, ugly, destructive and draining for all parties. Until the inner landscape of the mind is cleared up then the outer landscape will never change, and you will create the unwanted.

Embrace your skin, unhealed shame and let the light in…

The more love you send to your body, the more it will love you back. That is how it works, where attention goes, energy flows. Your meat bodysuit requires physical exercise to bring those thoughts into action, as this is not about wishful thinking. You have to do the inner work with purposeful action as your life is full of miracles fluff is spiritual bullshit. Nothing happens by non-action. I don't resonate with all of Wayne Dyer teachings, yet this resonates with natural law.

Ask, are your thoughts loving and kind or they harming you?

> 'Change your thoughts and change your life'. - Dr. Wayne Dyer

You have all been there as either the one saying what is wrong with your body or hearing another complaining about their body. Soon you start looking at that part and think, is there something not normal about it and you question the beauty you originally saw.

Stop getting in your little groups and partaking in bitching and complaining about things that you do not like by talking about others unkindly and stop comparing yourself to others. Each time you come into agreement with another that is of a complaining and bitching frequency, such things like entities jump and can easily attach to you. Oops! You invite their karmic shit storm, and the lessons will follow for you to take ruthless responsible action on.

Complaining is a disease of humans and is rewarded by a victim consciousness within society.

When friends do it:

- Change the subject
- Get up and walk away
- Pull them up with love!
- Make space for others to find you.
- Do not entertain it, be discerning with your words.
- Think and choose wisely who you are sharing time with.
- Take responsibility for your part in the collective karmic mess.

These friends are feeding your stuck-ness and are teachers in disguise. By entertaining it you are sending negative vibes all through your body and out into the universe. I see this as a major reason to why many women and men are single, for they are still complaining about their last relationship. These people want the relationship yet need to begin with themselves. The relationship is revealing what you are ready to see, and honor within self!

> *"I am me, I don't have a choice, from the time I accepted myself, everything got brighter. People were attracted to me for me".* - Queen Latifah

No one body is the same, and especially when we get to the topic of Yoni's. All are unique in glory, like beautiful wildflowers. This is the same for the lingam (Sanskrit term for penis). All come in many different shapes, sizes and beautiful unique forms. Even the taste is unique, the natural allure of the pheromones mixed with sweat is all different and will change according to the inner vibration of the soul and body hair. I will be honest, the more bodies I have seen, the greater my appreciation for my body canvas.

There is something naturally sensual and mesmerizing about a naked woman, I truly understand why men see true beauty in her nakedness, beyond shape or size. This is sensual appreciation in the most natural essence, and way beyond sexual seduction that many have been subjected to. The more women I have sensually massaged over the years whilst guiding their partner, the more I fall in love with how divine we truly are. Each layer is unique with textures, colour and responses. Observing a woman opening into her unapologetic sensual wholeness and giving herself permission to let go beyond performance is magical and an honour to support in a healing session.

A Holy temple, designed by Nature / Source/ God

Variety and diversity are the spice of life.

Different Name for the Female Genitalia?

Time for some lightness and fun to ruffle up some tethered feathers as this is a great icebreaker to soften the edges and get all the names out there. Have fun with this, get playful and express the playful recesses of the mind as all words are welcome. Take off the hat of correctness, relax and get the whole family to play (teenagers). It is a great icebreaker for 13-years onwards. Well, it was in our household.

Here are a few I came up with or heard over the years.

Fanny, vag, fur burger, bacon-buttie, gibblets, beaver, pussy, snatch, love tunnel, paradise, money slot, kitty, pom-pom, inner sanctuary, sacred kingdom, and yes, Cunt. It is the time to illuminate a word that is seen as the most vile, vulgar and offensive C-word.

The word Cunt is considered to be the most obscene and vulgar swear word in the English language, yet the word *Cunt* in the vernacular, means vagina. As if that is not indication enough why it is considered so vile a term in the vagina-hating patriarchy. The word itself was originally a term of respect and reverence for a powerful and spiritually enlightened woman.

The word 'cunt', which is usually used in society to degrade a woman, I used to think that it was the patriarchal men that created this, yet there are always two sides to any story.

I personally feel that there was a group of women that created shame around the women that were free in sensual embodied essence. She was seen as a temptress, wild, free, untamed, and lusted after by men, and secretively by women. The Feminine that was tapping into the Source feminine Goddess essence proper to this was manipulating men with this sacred power and using men as sperm donors, lustful pleasure at their disposal and having no respect for the masculine form. There is nothing new, and what goes too much one way will bounce back the other like the pendulum, attempting to harmonise and balance. One of the principles of being human is to unify the masculine and feminine energies and understand the polarities that play out within Self and the universe. It is up to each individual to discern and to align with right choices with the knowledge known and to know what is right and what is wrong. To never take from another's property (body, freedom, sovereignty) as theft is theft. This inner Source power is powerful and requires wise discernment and integrity.

What if is this offensive term was created by the patriarchy to keep their women happy by 'slut shaming' thus creating an illusion of security in their relationship? To shame her was a way of making excuses for their husband's lustful desires and to lessen her value? The ugly competitiveness within women is still rampant in society. I am on a mission to bridge the gap. I know how it feels to be uncomfortable around sexually confident women and I have explored all sides. What I most resisted and rejected was what I secretly desired within. What I most feared was my own raw feminine source power, a gift to be unleashed, embraced and honoured.

DIVINE SOURCE GODDESS

By hiding the 'wild free woman' away from the public eye, she became the object of lustful desires and I feel this is where shame, guilt and sin and rage towards feminine sexuality began. Rage for many has marinated over time and it is my mission to assist to transmute rage, dissolve delusions and expose what's beyond the veil of the illusion. The women were free in feminine innocence and she was misused, abused and her sacred power fed off. Perhaps, this is where the sex industry began?

The word cunt is derived from the name for one of the Great Oriental Goddesses; *Cunti* or *Kunda,* the *Yoni of the Universe.* The word represents beauty, power, and the amazing ability of the female body to bring new life into the world. From the same name the words country, 'Kin' and 'kind' came from.

The word *Cunti in Sanskrit* means a small well or reservoir. This is very fitting to this magical ocean of life and Yoni-niverse.

The word *Yoni* translates to *a sacred place and the source of all life.* A divine passage from where all life comes and to where all life returns for renewal. Every building has arch ways, doorways, entrances which represent the sacred pathway of the feminine Source portal.

Begin to be kind and loving towards your flowering yoni by sending yoni-love to her. Celebrate uniqueness in get to know your body, then way she likes to be touched, teased and pleasured are different for each woman. Sensual healing is taking place to shift from sexual to sensual and from shame to freedom. The name of this book almost became Cunti and it was in a pause in the process that I realised it would alienate those that didn't understand the true meaning were the ones who needed to read the book.

Shocking people had been a theme since I walked at 8 months old, and I've learnt it's not always the best way to impact and invite change. Thankfully, I have softened into my feminine inner power beyond the masculine force of noise.

What is/are your favorite name(s)?

Do you have a special name and what does your partner like to call this amazing wonder? It depends on the setting and the intimate moment, right!? Words are to be used contextually, so is using the anatomical name 'vagina' for pap smears is appropriate and more recently, 'yoni.'

It is time for women to step into her Goddess Source Self and to stop hiding. Begin to embrace your confidence as a sensually aware and curious woman. These all-un-leash creative life force fluids to pursue your sensual inner mystery which is self-soothing. A path to leading you into the realm of sacred sensuality. This starts with internal alignment where you create new attitudes about sex, sensuality and your body parts. To be discerning and selective who you choose to share those intimate desires and the timing of choices. Sensual arousal begins in the mind and much of society live highly stressed lifestyles which dampen natural and healthy sexual responses, sensuality and intimacy is nervous systems connecting.

DIVINE SOURCE GODDESS

It is time to embrace your divine feminine, she is healing, life-giving, transforming, sacred and creative. Sensual pleasuring can be experienced by both men and women to keep the love connection juices alive within relationships. – Zoe-Anna

From learning to love my own body and perceived flaws I began to honor all sensual desires and appreciation of men and women's form as each a tapestry of art. We are each erotic and unique art-forms, and the feminine form is a gift waiting to be un-wrapped. Start to embrace what you have been blessed with and get ready to see with loving eyes. I may have said this before, yet when I repeat take note as it is a love note for your soul of glowing-golden wisdom. Self-love and acceptance begin and ends within.

The goddess within is to be adored, celebrated and honoured by all. Invite the men in your life to recognise the potency of his own Divine feminine. Women through time have been suppressed, dishonored and disempowered, yet women are still buying into the pleasing game, all to please their partner, and ignore their own needs. Men too are experiencing this, as they may feel obliged to please her sexually even when he is not really feeling like it. This is a vital piece of wisdom to share with teenagers, soul sisters and brothers to remember who they are. This is not about finding something outside of self, this is all about awakening a sacred potency within.

As I began writing my first book in 2015, one book on my bookshelf caught my eye. *Reclaiming Goddess Sexuality* - by Linda E Savage

This book had been sitting on my shelf for years. I would walk past it every day and then one day was inspired to pick it up. Initially, I was triggered by the term, Crone. Little did I realise that the crone is a divinely wise sacred Goddess – a Spirit leader! It is interesting how words impact perception, cloud clear seeing of a deeper message calling to your Soul to explore.

The Three Faces of the Goddess

Linda goes into the three faces of the Goddess that we move through, as a woman, Aphrodite, Gaia and Isis in *Reclaiming Goddess Sexuality*.

APHRODITE The Free Maiden

Goddess of love, beauty and exploring her sexual creativity.

The first face of the ancient goddess is the Maiden. Represented by Aphrodite, the goddess of creative energy and sexual love. Aphrodite was called the virgin, as she is a woman without ties to any male. She was portrayed as athletic, intelligent and clever. She is the most sexually adventurous of the Greek Goddesses and had many lovers, with a creative sexual power. It is her quality of freedom, to choose partners as well as her creative expression that makes her a worthy choice as an archetype for the Maiden to discover creativity and explore sexuality.

Within this stage the individual is developing creative potential, through learning by exploration of sexual pleasure without the burden of motherhood. There is unlimited sexual activity where she is free to discover for herself, with wise guidance, her role in sexual pleasure and her unique limits. The maiden stage ends with pregnancy and the birth of her first child.

For women who never bare children much of her service is giving to children and sharing wisdom, guidance and often their creative talents. Seeing all of Earths children as her own, with so much love to give them. Such as working with children and guiding them, as in teaching.

GAIA- THE EARTH MOTHER

Responsibility of the Mother is protecting and nurturing her young.

Gaia is the Greek word for *Earth*. The image of earth mother represents the view that authority means the acceptance of responsibility for the well-being of the people. She protects, nurtures and cares for her own. It is the transition from maiden to mother, where new feminine characteristics emerge. Giving birth, is the ultimate creative art and a profound change that compels women to shift into the mother stage by accepting responsibility for another human life in their charge. It is also about letting go and trusting. Her development task is about accepting responsibility with a huge surge of hormones and fierce emotions of protection that are about ensuring the well-being of her baby comes first. The shift in consciousness that takes place with her first baby is the most sudden and powerful in life. I recall very primitive instincts taking over my body at the birth of my first and I called this phase the *Lioness Instinct,* where for the first few days only you and your partner hold the baby. It is vital to give a mother this bonding skin to skin opportunity. Unless you've been there, it is hard to comprehend, the need to protect and hold close that precious life. Anyone who tries to get in the way gets pushed aside, so to many it may look a little crazy. *My baby*, it is the most natural instinct so never feel wrong for acting on your instinct for survival. Give the new mother and baby space to move through this. It is a very scared time of bonding for the new mother and the baby she has carried within her for nine to ten months.

If this doesn't show up with the first, then give some huge attention to the mother, as it is natural to be overprotective initially.

There may be something else, like the mum being deeply nourished too. Spiritually, it is a beautiful journey teaching the deeper meaning of surrender through the overpowering body processes at work. The responsibility of the mother constantly put to the test, patience and lessons of compassion and unconditional love. Any mother may still go through this with her children. What an empowering process the entire pregnancy and birthing process is, so much sweet opportunity to let go and surrender to a greater force with full trust and faith in the power of nature.

Shifting in consciousness form self to selfless compassion- for another human being.

For those early years everything is given over to her child, sleep, body, attention and her entire existence must be given over to her child. Surrender and compassion are deep spiritual lessons that carry over into her sexuality. It is important during this time to take some time to step-away and fill-up on you, for your sanity and growth as a woman, as you have desires, dreams and passions. Let's be honest, for many this may not mean being at home with the children all day covered in vegemite and jam smeared on your clothes up to the ears in nappies and having creative play time with toddlers. We are each unique, gifted and special in our own way, and it is okay to step away and have some space.

Children are gifts, and the time we have with them when they are young is precious and very small in the grand scheme of our lives.

ISIS: Return of the Queen

The Goddess of awakening, wise teacher, spiritual healer of mind- body and spirit.

Isis demonstrated a perfectly balanced life as a great spiritual teacher and devoted wife and mother to (Osiris and Horus, respectively). She is a much-revered Egyptian goddess who symbolizes feminine strength and power. The Queen of Heaven with the Egyptian name for their most revered Goddess. Her symbols were the serpent, which represents feminine powers, empowerment and divination; and wings, associated with the mysteries of death and rebirth.

Isis the Goddess, the mother and the giver of life

Isis resembles the Crone woman because she exemplifies qualities of crone wisdom combined with high spiritual authority. Psychic visionary, dream interpretation, divine healing and inspired guidance. The association with the serpent, the snake also represents Kundalini, which is the Vedic term for sexual energy, used for sexual healing in the sacred practices of the *Temple Priestesses.*

Isis reminds us about our need for occasional renewal and reconnection in our relationships. Isis also reminds us to acknowledge and accept the depths of our emotions.

Each goddess stage is organized around blood mysteries.

1. The onset: menarche, (2) childbirth, blood from birthing and (3) menopause, when a woman's wise blood remains inside her to give her wisdom. They function as psychological gateways to the change in consciousness required by each new stage.

The Development Task of the Crone

She is a source of wisdom where others seek her counsel for important decisions. A heightened awareness of human nature and great insight, spiritually this is the master phase. The wise woman teaches knowledge gained from her education and life experiences. It is a time of utilizing her powers of intuition and finding meaning from her visions from the dreamworld, often many becoming masters of healing at the highest level. The change from mother to crone is a more gradual psychological shifting than from maiden to mother. It is impossible to use the cessation of the menses as the definition for this stage because it may take months to several years for a woman to realize that she has had her last one. The crone stage is a time of giving back to society, all the wisdom cumulated over the years. She is speaking up, organizing others and taking positive action. She is on her life path, with an urge to teach others and cultivate her passions. It is the most productive time in a woman's life.

Sexually this is a potentially powerful one, the stage of sexual mastery. Crone woman's continued sexuality in ancient times is one of the unknown mysteries. Some older women chose to stay sexually active with their ageing mates. If widowed or unattached, they are known to take younger male lovers for pleasure.

Crone sexual response is no longer estrogen dependent, as in the maiden and mother stages it is not limited by the cycles of progesterone as with mother pregnancy and birth.

It is all the potential power that comes from the will of a fully conscious, self-reliant, experienced, self-knowing and wise woman. A woman may reach this phase before her periods cease and evolve into the wise woman that she is. If she chooses, she can use her sexuality to serve a higher purpose by receiving divine inspiration and connecting to source.

This is the wholeness that most have forgotten, the sacred union of the sacred masculine and divine feminine within self, the divine union and self-reliant from any other external form. The birthing of the golden child.

Spiritual and sexual energy can be channeled into art on any subject as those creative juices flow and originate from the same source energy or Godliness. I embrace the crone as she exemplifies the phase I am living and celebrate my crimson moon flow in my own sacred offering in private ceremony.

In 2019, I chose celibacy until I was met by a sacred masculine. A man that embodied his wholeness, stripped himself bare of his labels, and is walking his aligned path of soul potency. This lasted 9 months as I did take a younger lover on the rare occasion, yes, a 48-year-old woman and a 29-year-old masculine. In this deep sensual mind-body connection, age and time became less relevant. I felt this was passing on feminine wisdom and enjoyed his desire to connect deeply by undressing my mind, as I guided him into deeper states of ecstasy. What was required was a deeper understanding of the feminine, and this is why it is vital to empower and guide women, so she can lead him deeper into himself. It is insane as even my memory is now blank from my canvas of the event. In 2020, diving deeper into self and choosing celibacy until May 2021. To transcend the physical act of sexual interweaving and take sensuality into magical states of pure divinity.

I am here to serve and share wisdom. Labels have become meaningless, and I've let go of titles of status that I once held onto. Many use titles for some kind of hierarchy, a desire for power and control, perhaps this is an aspect to the toxic feminine. Labels such as Higher Priestess, Empress, and even Goddess, in an attempt for status and self-recognition.

I am what I am, pure divine existence of Source as the light of grace. The greater the labels the greater the ego distortion thirsty for power recognition of the title.

Rise as the embodied & awakened SHE

See Your Beauty Within

There is no need to hide

I've seen you before

I've been in your shoes

Held hostage by perceived flaws

Imprisoned by your fears

Misguided thoughts

Inner separation

Keeping us apart.

I am here now

It's safe and it's okay

To remove the mask

It served you well

You are stunningly beautiful

It's time to see

All that I see

And all that you are

To reveal your inner beauty

Hiding within.

WILDFLOWER

Take my hand

And let's play together

To be free within

A new field of possibility

Adventures and opening

Encapsulated in one

I will be your courage

Your honesty

Motivation, inspiration

And a warm space

To no longer run.

Simply close your eyes

As they distort your truth

Tainted by misperception

Your infection within

As only the truth

Rests within your heart

You will find me there

Waiting for your return

DIVINE SOURCE GODDESS

Your loyal servant

You are the master

All along

I am you and

I am love

I will never leave

Even if you forget

All that your desire

I will be there, infinite within.

Chapter 2: The Designer Vagina

> *"What makes you vulnerable makes you beautiful"*
>
> - Brené Brown

Yoni Healing

This topic began as a powerful message to be expressed fearlessly and shamelessly on stage in 2015. A journey un-folding as I gave a public talk about 'The Rise of The Designer Vagina'. This was the catalyst to sharing my story so fewer girls and women felt the pressure to get cut and healthy flesh removed.

In Breaking Free, I expressed how at 12 years of age I felt trapped in shame, disgusted in my body with the horrific contemplation of removing healthy flesh from my Labia. I desperately wanted an *innie* as I thought that was 'normal', and like what I saw in porn magazines. Thankfully, I never proceeded and today remain uncut with healthy pink vulval flesh.

Many women feel or have felt in their life that their yoni is ugly?

In this chapter, I will also refer to the yoni as the designer vagina.

Do You feel bad about your body, sending unkind and mixed messages to sensitive areas that you don't like? You're not alone. For many women and teenage girls, it has become a daily destructive habit of self-hate.

The yoni is beautiful and vulnerable that hears and feels the energy you send it. When the attention is negative this can lead to an unhappy and depressed Wildflower. Each cell in your body experiences each and every emotion as it is bathed 24/7 by them. Awareness around this concept is vital and it is key to pay close attention to this message and pay it forward to your children and teenagers. Risky behaviours like taking sexy pictures, are erotic and exciting at the time, yet are now out there for all to view on the dark web. It is time to bring awareness and protect those we love. It begins with self-love and self-acceptance beyond external validation from others and to forgive yourself from mistakes you have made in regard to this sensitive topic.

For women going through the often dreaded, yet powerful transition into menopause, the sensitive inner lining of the vagina can become thinner and dry. This can cause sensitivity and irritation so connecting with her mind and entire body is key. No matter the goddess stage in life, it is our human right to feel sensual and free in expression. I have found organic coconut oil to be a great lubricant when giving the delicate tissues of the yoni a self-massage. This is explored later in the book, restoring healthy sensuality through healing rituals (Chapter 6)

'Your ability to concentrate and focus is connected to natural sensual arousal. It is meditation that juices the mind to naturally open your wildflower as the mind gets out the way'. Zoe Bell

FACING A FEAR WIDE OPEN

In 2016, a female sensuality body therapist invited me to be the model for a sensual massage demonstration attended by fifteen men. I was an attendee of the weekend course, and the previous day I had thought, *I wonder who the model is?* In the back of my mind thinking, I hope I get asked.

This would be a pivotal point in my healing journey around sensuality and pave the way for my Soul mission as a healer as the universe is always listening!

The experience was beautiful. I felt safe, loved, and held in healing space. My body was excited, nervous with anticipation of the unknown. I was facing one of my greatest fears, that of being exposed and seen. My heart was pounding as the silky robe gently slide towards the floor exposing my full naked essence. The coolness of the room touches my flesh, catching my breath as my intimate rawness exposed with 17 pairs of attentive eyes gazing upon. Shaking all over, I was guided to focus on my breath to relax into calmness. I was met with love all in one: it was intoxicatingly beautiful the depth of love that I felt. *Wow and triple wow!* To be seen beyond sexual gratification or lustful desires was healing.

A deep level of trust and connection of intimacy was established with the setting of boundaries, and the space created for me to drop into this safe container. I learned that I had no idea of what boundaries were, and how to express them, until that moment. It was on this day, that I began to re-claim my No, and my inner power of choice to own my fuck-yes!

As I lay on the massage table I was guided deeper into the breath. Trusting and letting everything go and navigating inwards. A magical journey to opening and allowing the inner healing. I was touched only by the facilitator, gentle touches over my skin, my thighs, my breasts, my whole body. A soft remembrance, I had been yearning and longing for. My yoni gently touched, the labial tissues massaged, stretched and my entire body experienced waves of sensual warm energy surging. As the sacredness of my feminine energy opened, the men opened into a steady tenderness. I held nothing back, I felt safe to seen, guided and supported by the facilitator. She guided the men in observation mode how to perform the different touches, stretches and stroke methods. At moments, my labia opened wide, full pinkness on full view as I melted into deep relaxion.

At the end, I was met with waves of *ecstatic bliss*. As I gazed around smiling, repeating the phrase, Thank You. That feeling of sensual bliss, even though I did not climax, the experience was simply divine. Directed to lay back down beyond the external distraction of thanking everyone, to let it all go, relax and allow. As my eyes closed my entire body was overcome with intense love and gratitude. As the warm blanket was pulled up over me, I was overcome in waves of suppressed emotional pain mixed with the pure pleasure, simultaneously exploding in my body. It was like a warm bear hug that felt safe. I trusted the process and like a volcano erupting as I unleashed into deep sobbing of my own neurosis. Warm salty tears stung upon pink flushed cheeks as I embraced the sacred stillness, I lay there crying rivers of grief and the many years of self-loathing and shame. This began the journey in healing sensuality and the freedom to be unapologetically me.

Tears shifted into joy, acceptance, restored courage and a new vocabulary to loving myself. To feel loved, accepted and honored as a woman in all her raw vulnerable beauty in the presence of the masculine.

Potent, raw vulnerability in motion.

Sensual freedom, pure love and inner peace is your human right as men and women. Life lessons are infinite. Each experience magical, guided by curiosity as all the lessons are within the experience. It is choice how to see it.

The softening of my hardened edges of warrior protection, began to drop away over the years and the canvas of the past now wiped blank from deep womb healing in August 2020. It is magical to guide sisters and brothers in restoring sacred sensuality to meet eye to eye, heart to heart, sacral to sacral in deep love and mutual respect.

> *"I see a beautiful wildflower in full bloom, magical in expression with subtle tones of pink arousal. Her divine glory, a mystery opening with no force. Her magical lips that gaze in joyful bliss. She is a pure vessel of cosmic light, Amrit her sweet nectar of life. She is sovereign, her body a sacred flowering mystery of the holy temple".* Zoe Bell

Nature by design, each fold of flesh a gift of God's creation.

Removing Healthy Tissue

It is time to recognise and remember that you are perfect the way you are. You are each beautiful and unique creations of Source/God in your full goddess and godliness. You have been given bodies to learn important life lessons for which you came here to experience a human life. It is time to wake up from the illusion created by the media and the sad fact that many teenage girls are modelling themselves off mega celebrity superstars. This is all falsely created and NOT real life. They are part of another ploy to numb, dumb and hypnotise you into thinking, *you are not good enough, pretty enough or rich enough!* Everything about it is plastic and fabricated, even playing on the fact of acting dumb, which I am sure they are not. All playing a role in the illusion the media will feed you. It is not who they are, it is the puppets they are playing all to dumb the masses down, even further.

The issue is low self-esteem and the way you choose to see yourselves.

I see all too often as many teenagers and adults struggle with low self-esteem. I had plastic surgery with bilateral breast augmentation at 30 years old, and this was a band-aid for my low self-esteem. I was obsessed by tits from a very young age. Then influenced by what was seen in the lingerie and pornographic magazines. It is crazy how any woman that natural reveals labial contours in her lingerie is visually altered to conform in magazines, as it is seen as offensive. Yet for a guy, he gets extra padding in his underwear, with full contours in full view to add to his power. The shame is right there!

Women are being digitally castrated, and men are accentuated.

Can you imagine what would happen in society if a man in a magazine had his testicles removed? His flesh snipped off with one click, and oops, testicles gone. Men, I am sure You would agree, this is a massive wake-up.

A man without balls would cause public outrage, right?

Welcome to the 'eunuch'

According to the urban dictionary: 'A eunuch is a man whose balls have been removed either for government service (such as in ancient Africa and Roma) or, if the castration takes place before puberty, to prevent the voice from breaking (Italian Opera's male sopranos of the 17th Centuries). In the present day, this sort of eunuch may be a result from testicular cancer.'

Testicular cancer awareness and early detection is vital for teenage boys from the age of 15 years to 30 years old. Make it a habit to feel and examine your testicles in the shower at least once every month.

WILDFLOWER

Testicles are vital and very important for procreation, as are Vulvas!

About 50% of the population has innies, and the other 50% outies, Labiaplasty, is No different from Female Genital mutilation. This means 50% of women have Labia Minora, that extend beyond the margin of the labia Majora, but that is not what we see advertised and, in the media.

F.G.M, Female Genital Mutilation is the removal of healthy tissue that gives the woman sexual power and a healthy response to fully enjoy pleasure. It denies her the pleasure and gives the power over to the man. It is barbaric, horrific and evil. Not to mention the damaging effects of the trauma from the surgeon's knife and the years of self-loathing and self-hatred in the tissues of the yoni. This can create much blocked flow of energy and unhealthy sensual and reduced sexual healthy response.

According to the Sydney Morning Herald "The female genital surgery conspiracy" March 07, 2013, stated that; In the last decade, images of women's genitals have become widely available on the Internet, adult magazine's and in some women's publications. But many of these images are totally unrealistic and don't depict normal variations.

Labiaplasty is on the rise!

Society it has become more about aesthetics of what they think is normal to loving and embracing our yoni uniqueness. Thanks to the bullshit mind manipulating media and the distractions of the rich and famous in the trashy magazines. Much of what we see in magazines is not real, it is airbrushed, or photo shopped to look more acceptable.

WHAT IS LABIAPLASTY?

ABC TV documentary on labiaplasty, 'The Vagina Diaries' shines a light on the increasing number of women choosing to go under the knife to have their labia removed, writes Rebecca Deans, Published 'The Conversation', Nov 27, 2013.

UNSW Gynecologist Dr. Rebecca Deans explains labiaplasty.

"Labiaplasty, is where the Labia Minora, which are the inner lips of the vagina are somehow reduced or altered surgically. Many people refer to the external part of the genitalia as the vagina where in fact it is the Vulva. The vagina is a tube that is not really visible from the outside. The main features of the vulva are the four labia or lips. The two outer ones are called the Labia Majora and the two smaller labia the Labia Minora. It is very common to have protruding inner labia, with one longer than the other, saying they are too long and too ugly. Some believe that by having them surgically altered and reduced in size, will make them look normal again.

I personally have the view that this is sensitive and healthy tissue full of vital nerve endings for healthy arousal and sensual pleasure in a woman. I know many women that have had it, some regret it, and some are really happy with the result. In life, everything is choice, and I am sharing a perspective on this topic. I feel this is about restoring healthy body image, self-love and self-acceptance to address the insecurities amongst teenagers and women as surgery is not the solution.

Clinical Sexologist in Melbourne, Dr. Frances D-Arcy-Tehan. A PhD candidate at the University of Sydney. Her thesis: Genital image and body image and sexual functioning in women. Was published in the Sydney morning Herald, March 7th, 2013, talking the Designer Vagina.

"The healthy tissue of the labia Minora is a highly sensitive sexual organ and plays an important role for sexual response. It is dense with nerve endings and sensory receptors, which are highly sensitive to light touch. The main function of the vulva is to give pleasure and the labiaplasty has the obvious potential to destroy an erogenous zone and can lead to lack of arousal and impede orgasmic response." - Dr. Frances D-Arcy-Tehan

THE BARBIE DOLL VAGINA

This is not a topic any healthy minded adult wants to talk about. It is a conversation that may trigger an inner reaction, of what the f#ck! Globally, many young and older women are hijacked by the idea of this designer style 'tight vagina'. I was sitting in a lavish area of Eastern Sydney and overheard a group of 55 years+ women talking about their upgraded young *slit-like vagina's*. This barbie doll style vagina is that of an 8-year-old vagina, a 12-year-old and even being asked by the cosmetic surgeon, which age vagina would your husband prefer!? Like WTF!

Aesthetics and tonality based on the representation of a child's vagina & tightness. This has nothing to do with a healthy pelvic floor and learning how to activate the inner muscles for sensual intimate connection. It was all about the physical mechanics of penetration and desires of the man.

What fascinated me about these women is them getting vaginas to look like their child-like self so their partner or husband with a possibly more-wrinkly penis, could put his willy inside their vagina. I almost vomited. This is a huge concern, a massive pink elephant in the room moment. This is to increase awareness to think twice if you are still contemplating going in to get tidied up. All to look like an eight or twelve-year-old, this sounds like alarm bells to me!

This got me asking the questions?

- Are we creating more monsters in society, who prey on young and innocent children as they feel an un-healthy lust for the woman in the magazine who would be unavailable?

- Are barely teens being used for sensual shoots dressed up in an adult fashion magazine as to feed the lustful desires of men?

These sick perverts take children, dress them up, put make-up on them, to re-create what they see and feel lust towards an innocent child, in a very sick way. Those that prey on children are obsessed and addicted to feeding off the pure lifeforce energy of a child. When we look at sensuality, it is pure life-force energy that we are re-learning how to access within self. For many it has been fed off, manipulated and abuse through over-sexualisation of children, and hence why we have so many lost souls in society. In 2020, much more is now being publicly revealed where children throughout history have been bred underground, used, misused, abused and sacrificed for sick sexual and perverted satanic rituals. Those that courageously stand for truth and justice will say this, it is all for saving the children and reclaiming innocence.

Babies are being sexually abused by having their exposed circumcised penis kissed by Catholic priests and children's innocent minds highjacked with ideas of gender confusion and from how they play and explore with different toys. These are seeds of nefarious new world order intentions being planted and here it is again, de-humanisation and de-sensitisation with an attack on pure innocence using mind-fuckery.

Let's not create more distortions into the equation by opting for bodies modification and ideology to that of a child. Embrace your body, love every inch of your skin and stop feeding this cosmetic service of bullshit. This book is about remembering and restoring what is within, and to reclaim your sensual innocence, as this is your sacred sensual lifeforce. It is how you begin to heal You.

Has society become too focused on aesthetics rather than pelvic floor strength?

Pelvic floor strengthening and inner healing over labial image.

The inside walls of the vagina are muscular, spongy and warm. By sending unhappy and destructive thoughts to your body will create an unhappy, toxic and angry environment. Yes, emotions have a direct impact on the sensual fluids and natural response of the body. Can you begin to see that energetics and a healthy sensual connection in self is far more important that aesthetics. In fact, men report that they enjoy the engorged labial lips as it adds to the sensation around the shaft of his penis (lingam) during love making. Rather than focus on aesthetics focus on functionality, sensation, energetic resonance, and strength. A vulva is like a mouth and lips like to feel fleshy, that is my personal opinion. The inside of the vagina is the same texture as the inside of the mouth and vaginas are not meant to have teeth. I say that tongue in cheek to the women that are hurting men with unhealed and hungry vaginas.

Like flowers, each woman is divine and unique. A flower does not have to compete with another, and there is not one yoni better looking than the other. It is more vital to learn how to activate the deep muscles within your vagina as its structure is designed much like that of an accordion and so when you are inviting another into your sacred temple, you can lengthen, milk and squeeze very naturally. It is vital to learn how to massage the deep clitoral tissues that are deep in the body around and beneath the vulva and guide your partner. This increases yoni engorgement and enjoyment in sensual activity for both as the inside walls of the vagina swell and become snug, warm and engorged with light.

For many men and women there is still unresolved and stuck trauma in the labial tissue. No amount of surgery will reverse the trauma, in fact, the surgery will add to the scar tissue and create further trauma to healthy tissues. These tissues need loving attention to assist sensually healing as much touch has become sexually orientated where many have become numb, disconnected and disassociated.

It is time to heal the sensitive tissues of the yoni rather than creating more dysfunction and to be guided by resonance and activation over aesthetics. We have enough faces on the planet that don't move, let's not further desensitise healthy flesh. This is explored in Chapter 6: Restoring Healthy Sensuality with Healing Rituals.

A CULTURAL CONTRAST

In Africa, the Labia are celebrated and the longer the labia the more honour you bring to your family. It is part of their culture to sit in groups and perform certain practices to elongate one another's labia. When the girls are ready to be married, if their labia are not elongated enough, they will bring shame on their family.

The men report, that the longer and more engorged the labia the better the sex, more stimulation & pleasure for both man and women. Different cultures have very different opinions on the women's genitals. They celebrate luscious labia.

Apparently, I have been told my yoni is like that of the Ancient Egyptian women. Cleopatra apparently had swollen inner labia and a voluptuous yoni. Hail the fat flapped vulva.

F.G.M is still practiced globally and is a violation of human rights of girls and women. With more awareness and empowering our children, I feel we can each make a difference.

POSITIVE AWARENESS IN THE MEDIA

Melinda Tankard Resit, a media commentator and author of Big Porn Inc. and Getting Real- Challenging the sexualization of girls, believes pornography is a big driver in the rise in cosmetic surgery. I would agree and many of you may have had this experience.

> *"Girls are made to feel inadequate and think there's something wrong with their perfectly natural healthy bodies, and boys are expecting girls to provide the porn star experience".* - Ms. Resit

Ms. Resit. ads that it is important women pass on positive body image messages to their daughters, and that cosmetic surgeons should play their part by refusing to operate on very young women, rather than capitalizing on the body angst of girls" - Daily telegraph, Oct 2012 'The rise of the designer vagina'.

Cosmetic surgeons and other health professionals, who perform surgeries, play on the insecurities of women. What women are seeing in the media is also playing on their self-esteem, do I look sexy, attractive and young enough, it is a multi-billion-dollar industry.

According to the Sydney Morning Herald report 'The female genital surgery conspiracy'

"Many consumers when they approach cosmetic surgery companies are depressed or on medication and in some cases being sold operations without preliminary access to alternative psychological therapies. The advertising industry manipulates the consumer by campaigns that seduce the consumer."

The lingerie industry also uses younger models; I interviewed a lady who was an assistant of a large modelling casting agency, and here is what she said:

"The average age of the model is fourteen and fifteen years old- targeting an audience that is twenty-eight and thirty-four years of age."

They have their parents with them as they are minors and men are looking at these models, to buy underwear from their partners, they could easily be your daughter and something to ponder in regard to inviting over-sexualisation of teenagers.

An Ex-PA to a highly influential and successful lingerie company; during an interview with me she expressed how the images pre-digital alterations looked totally different. The women looked like women, where you may have seen a slight bulge from her womanliness, a bit too much of detail. All photo-shopped and made to look very un-realistic.

There are Lingerie brands that are shifting; They will not use any altered images of models. Instead, real girls and women, who happen to be skinny. It is a positive step forward and really refreshing to see clothing brands stopping the digital improved images, it will be even better when the models, are of any different sizes and shapes.

Take a moment to tune in and listen, as there will be plenty of opportunity to release and adapt to a new way of thinking as you go through this yoni healing journey. These tools can be applied if you are a man or woman.

- Are you unhappy with perceived imperfections?
- Are you unhappy in the skin you are in?

Each day, I embrace and love every inch of this vessel, embrace cellulite as it comes and goes, the shifting contours of my skin and touch my body every day. The less negative self-talk and attention placed upon perceived imperfections, the more love and light I invite in. My weight fluctuates depending on the fluid in my body and if I focus on trying to lose weight, my body holds onto it. As I embrace it, so my body responds as a divine creation of beauty.

May this begin to change your perspective and see your beautiful yoni as something mystical and beautiful, like a rare orchid.

"You have been criticizing yourself for years, and it hasn't worked. Try approving of yourself and see what happens". - Louise L. Hay

The more You embrace one another and accept you then you begin to release shame around nudity. It is then that you begin to appreciate the whole bodysuit, beyond lustful desires. Your body, your choice and when another take's without asking, then that is theft. It is as simple as that!

Chapter 3: Hijacked by Comparison

"I had to grow to love my body. I did not have a good self-image at first. Finally, it occurred to me, I'm either going to love me or hate me. I chose to love myself and then everything kind of sprung from there. Things that I thought weren't attractive became sexy. Confidence makes you sexy". -Queen Latifah

Comparison Hostage

Each and every day you are tested with temptations of desire and mind-highjacked into comparing yourselves with others. It is a game, you have been fed lies, false programs and told that we are not good enough. This directly relates to self-esteem, self-worth and self-confidence. It is time to play the infinite game, beyond fear and control from external influences.

The media plays on it, thinking you need this next product all to be more beautiful and to stay looking young. At almost 50 I feel younger and classier than ever. It is to do with inner sensual radiance, feminine magnetism and a bodysuit that has been kept flexible and free to move.

In Sanskrit ancient teachings, your stretch marks from childbirth and your juicy long labia of internal irritation and discomfort arise from wishing you were different. This is known as *Dukha*, or suffering. How many of you on a daily basis beat up on yourself? Be honest.

Suffering is self-created and self-perpetuated. The only way to reverse dukha is to acknowledge it, see it, own it and take action, by loving what you dislike. To shift into *Sukha*, meaning freedom and to do the badass inner work.

Each experience of suffering is a doorway and a vital aspect to discover You. As you evolve you will become less concerned with your body and there will be a transition point of transparency with a morphing into crystalline light-beings.

She blooms unafraid in untethered messiness

Inner work is internal housekeeping, like how a plumber cleans pipes and drains out, to become un-stuck, clean and glowing with vessels of light.

The energy of the past is dense, carbon in nature and needs to be dissolved into a fluid and flexible substance that shifts with change. Energy that is adaptive to expand. Where there are blockages, your judgment is clouded, and thinking is ridged or foggy. This is where irritation occurs, and you notice imperfections in others. You, the judge, the overactive mind bound in fear and in self-destruct mode. Metabolism gets sluggish and your breathing becomes shallow, swimming in toxic ocean of acidity. Blockages restrict the ability to be fully open with your sensual partner and make releasing in climax challenging. You have to learn to trust and let go, and work through what is ready to be healed. Hell is staying bound in your neurosis of attempting to control everything around you and the illusion you are attached to.

Are you bound in a distraction away from the truth keeping you locked within an illusion, and thinking you are not good enough, pretty enough, or desired enough?

Every cell in your body changes every seven years', so your face today looks different to seven years ago, have a look back at your pictures. What do you see? There is a sense of who you think you are being tragically tied up in looks or appearances and when these natural changes happen, then you realise the attachment to the superficial things in life. The key is to age gracefully from the inside out, as your Spirit is infinite.

YONI FEEDBACK FROM THE MEN AND WOMEN

I was fascinated and pleasantly pleased by what men expressed when sharing rich and magical conversations with them, all about the pussy/yoni. They brought the beauty into what many women viewed as ugly. It was time to un-cover a raw truth spoken by men and women at the time, in 2016. The intention was to see if there was a correlation between opinion, age range and the exposure of porn with men and how this shifted different attitudes around the vagina experience. For the women it was less around porn, more on their attitudes they had around their attitudes towards their vagina and sensuality.

This was a blind study, and even though a relatively small field of study, what was provided was a distinct insight into a much bigger problem. Discretion and identities anonymous for maintaining confidentiality. Full disclosure was given on the context and purpose of the original book, The Adventures of Pinky Fairway and was granted for future publications.

A warm huge thank you to all the men that gave such positive feedback. A true impact you each hold in this world and even though it was sad that so many women had a blurred view, it was direct confirmation that every woman must read the Pussy TRUTH from Men. Ages are in brackets, and this was the opening and question:

'What was your first experience up close and personal with a vagina and can you describe it?'

(50's): I was more interested in the touch and feel of connecting with the woman- it was more about connection.

(50's): I thought it was a place South of Warez- it wasn't the focus.

(40's): The magazines had some mystery and curiosity there was an element of intrigue, and the bush was inviting. Now the fanny is exposed- so there is nothing left to the imagination and with bits removed, it's not for me!

(40's): I was looking at porn before and my first encounter was at 16, and I love juicy luscious lips- they are inviting, and they taste better. It was the porn of John Holmes and Robert Guiciani- Penthouse.

(40's): My first encounter with a pussy was in 6th Grade. The hormones were thriving. Friends of mine, girls that were friends were eighth graders, so the girls were starting to examine themselves to socially grow. We were in the backyard, and she showed me her pussy. It was beautiful I thought it looked like a flower, a rose flower. We would get together each year and do it again.

(40's): Attraction is not based on what you can see, even though men are visual creatures, when there is an intense attraction, a woman who is confident and sassy- you are both in the zone- consumed and overwhelmed with their beauty. How she looks down there is not important.

** Now if a woman is 10/10 but is self-conscious and always thinking about how she looks and about herself, she starts to look unattractive- you lose the zone and will start thinking there is something wrong down there.

(40's): I remember it being a beautiful pussy and my first thought was how much I loved the taste and feeling of it. In comparison to seeing one in a porn magazine there is no comparison. Pussies are a beautiful part of a woman's body, all unique and pornography completely degrades the beauty of it.

(Late 30's): I love vagina's and going down on my partner is the best thing ever. It is all about taste, smell and how she feels in my mouth and especially how she feels when we have sex. I can talk about Vagina's all day, and I have seen many different shapes and sizes, some are tucked away, and some have juicy lips. The thought of women having healthy tissue removed is horrific and fucking stupid. I never knew this was happening and it has to stop. I am happy to get up on stage and talk about this, as it has to stop.

(30's): Wow, it feels really warm and inviting and safe I was 18 years old. Being brought up catholic I never had porn in the house, my mates and I would go to strip joints to look at women. I would rather take a lady out who is wearing sexy clothes rather than looking straight at her naked body, it is adds to the pleasure and mystery. It adds to the excitement to then undress her and explore her body more.

(30's): Is that normal? Prior to seeing a real pussy up close I was looking at porn magazines and video. The models I realised were airbrushed and touched up. At the time, the first time I was so nervous and was more interested in the woman. Then I saw others closer and thought, this is a lot, "it's not tidy"

(Late 20's): It was really puffy and lots of it, I was really put off, where do I start? Instead of going down on her, I was 15, I wet my finger and pretended to lick her out by using my finger on her pussy, so it made a wet licking noise. I now love all shapes, sizes and diversity of pussies and I cannot understand men who do not like to eat pussy, it is the sexiest thing. I was looking at porn magazines before and have always been very sexual. Strip shows was a norm growing up.

(Early 20's): I was 13 years old, and I felt it was the ultimate, I expected it to be amazing and it was!" It felt so good, and I still love it.

(20's): I was fascinated and a bit perplexed, as she didn't look like anything in the magazines. I was really into her, so I just got to learn more about what a woman looks like and how different they all are.

(18-20): It was not as glamorous as what I saw in a magazine- I was disappointed.

- The way men viewed the pussy had much to do with the era they were born in and what they were exposed to growing up. For example, the porn they were watching or looking at.

- The most alarming part was that the younger guys were disappointed with what they saw, and having two boys, this was an alarming concern as a mother.

It is also about not learning from porn, it is more vital to connect with another human being on an emotional level, and yes, we are curious and explorative by nature! I am sure there are not many women that want to be treated like the women are in a porn movie and thinking that they have to act like the porn star to feel desired and to look sexy, and yet this is what many women and young girls think.

This was a small blind study for the women, and the question was written. Many had their guard up and I was met with resistance. There was secrecy, shyness, and many were reserved and embarrassed. I used the word pussy and VJJ with women and pussy did not go down too well! Looking back as this was 2016, it would now be best to use terms such as vagina or yoni and at the time I was pushing the boundaries. To the women that took part, thank you.

"What was your first experience with looking at your Pussy or VJJ?"

(Mid 20's): The girls that were fuller down there, were teased and laughed at in the showers and called sluts. Because their labia were fuller and longer, which meant they must be promiscuous and sleep around.

(Late 20's): It wasn't until I became a nurse that I saw how many different shapes there were.

(30's): I never gave it any thought

(30's): We would compare ourselves and one day my friend when we were 16 asked if she could send me a photo, to see if she was normal. I was a bit shocked and then said, sure.

(40's): I still look at myself in the mirror every day and now I like the way I am.

(40's): After having children I became less conscious of my body.

(50's): Why are we even talking about this and being so focused on what it looks like?

When I heard the *slut story comment* (20's) it cut like a knife as I can remember being at school and even though it was me doing the self-judging, I had heard other girls saying that labia that were longer was a sign of promiscuity and being a slut. I wonder how many women still feel so shut down in shame when it comes to this question?

Some women said that they have never paid much attention down there.

Many avoided the question; some had never looked in a mirror and a very few could give a full description of their pussy/yoni. I found this shocking, and if you have never taken a good look, then now is the time. With many women there is internal shame or worry from what they have heard from others.

Worry is like a virus, and it will follow you around and is a bitch to leave. Worry will hang around, drag you down with it, and if there is something worrying you, then take action and do something about it. Worrying is like a person who is drowning and is refusing to grab the rope to help themselves, it is an old habit that does not serve anyone. It is like fear that you ignore.

Fear is toxic and needs to be crushed for good, unless there is a car driving towards you and you have to move fast into safety, it has its places and yes fear is also a safety switch to get out fast. Fear of another being better than you, will keep you stuck in comparison. Having resistance to another worry and anxiety, may also be reflecting back an aspect within self that you are unaware of in the shadow aspects of self.

AESTHETICS OVER PERFORMANCE

Here is an example of the media paying way too much to how a girl looks, rather than her sporting ability and is blatant perversion. Here is a story of an amazing gymnast who became more known in the media for the attention of her genitals. This started to unravel where much shame and comparison created! Thanks to the misogynistic bureaucrats and the media.

The headline: *Muslim gymnast Farah Ann Abdul Hadi offends Islamists with "revealing" leotard- June 18, 2015.*

"Farah Ann Abdul Hadi blitzed the Southeast Asia Games last week bringing home six medals, including two gold for Malaysia. Not that the country's religious hardliners noticed the impressive tally- they were too busy looking at the 21-year old's vagina. The Federal MP went on to say that it is the responsibility of all Muslims regardless of gender to cover their *Aurat.*"

This is ridiculous that the focus was on her genitals, and not her amazing ability as a gymnast. The more you go down the rabbit hole of truth, you start to *see the real sick truth* and many making these rules who are in power and doing the exact opposite behind closed doors, boys clubs where women are also young children used in a derogatory manner, for sex and lustful pleasure. Hiding in shame and guilt and deflecting what they hide behind, placing blame on others. 2020, has been the year for global exposure and still there is more to expose in 2021 and beyond! It is time to wake-up, and for women to never feel shame for being a woman. It is time to guide young girls and teenage girls the same as well as get this message to your fellow goddesses and to your teenage boys becoming real men.

BODY CONFIDENCE

The eyes will see what they choose to see, and neuroscientists have found that the eyes see by the picture being formed on the brain and also by what you hear, as it is heard within the brain. The eyes are influenced by the perception to our past experiences, old belief systems and attitudes to life. Who you choose to listen to will impact what you see, as you will see only what you are focusing upon? Most people that have poor body image learn to disconnect from their bodies. For those who have challenges with overall body image, this may be a rapid wake-you up!

Poor body image = destructive thoughts = unsatisfied intimacy

How You feel on the inside is directly impacting your sexual desire. When you feel light and happy you want to shout it from the rooftops, and when you feel annoyed, pissed-off, you want to hide from the world. Neither are right or wrong ways to feel as the truth is found within the emotion. Perhaps, the way you are feeling is your conscience guiding you to unplug from others and nourish You rather than unconsciously feeding off them.

Here are ways to honour Your Sassy Soul

- Watch a funny movie
- Write poetry
- Eat chocolate for breakfast!
- Get out in nature
- Play music and dance
- Ride you bicycle and try no hands
- Meditate every morning
- Yoga and exercise
- Read a book
- Enjoy a glass of red wine
- Have a date with yourself
- Explore new places.
- Colour and draw
- Spend time alone
- Enjoy a bubble bath
- Share a bubble bath
- Book in a massage or a self-massage
- Dance naked

- Connect with those you love.
- Have a nap in the day and simply honour your silence

Having sex to feel good is not self-love. It is an unhealthy habit of co-dependency!

Let's explore some playful and fun ways to *instantly boost body-confidence*. This can be fun to do with a girlfriend, or your partner. I will say this as wind to caution, going to a nude beach by yourself initially, may not be a good idea as you may feel exposed and it is sad to say, an easy target for predator behaviour.

- Visit a nude beach
- Take a sauna naked
- Practice yoga naked, at home or at the beach.
- Join a naked yoga class
- Walk around your house naked and be free.
- Stand in front of the mirror and shake all your wobbly bits.

Your perception becomes your projection, so when you hear the inner critic, catch yourself and give your body love thoughts.

Wild and free Feminine Source within the feminine source.

"You are imperfect, permanently invisible and inevitably flawed. And you are beautiful".

-Amy Bloom

Enjoy this poem of the interweaving feminine forces of Mother Gaia dancing with the masculine forces, Father sky. Let us as all celebrate divine remembrance to honour the beautiful land and honour the magical garden within us all, a path to Eden.

A Spirit Prayer to our Native Lands

It is time to awaken those asleep

Honour the beautiful lands

Mother Earth and Father sky are calling to us

Holding us close, listening in

It is time to rise up!

Honour your bodies, your gifts

To step up and shine your light

Great spirit is calling.

Your indifferences dissolve into oneness

Each perfection within all its perceived imperfections

A difference in flavour in full expression

Glory of unique souls, expanded versions of God

It is time to unify our masculine and feminine

Forces, within and without

To dance freely within the karmic playing field of life

The energetic intertwining of the sacred dance

To release our sexual oppression to bring into the light

To embrace the dark and shadows with love

HIJACKED BY COMPARISON

Dissolving perceived separateness with peace

Our mystical allure - to discover One Love.

To restore & evoke ancient wisdom

and celebrate sexual free expression

Moving forward may we bring those energies into harmony

With effortless ease and divine grace

To flow within and without, all spaces in-between.

As Sacred Earth lovers and Soul-seekers

All living for a higher good, to serve humanity.

To express freely the potent omnipotent life force

Never hiding in shame again

To break free from the shackles of guilt

Exploring her deep valleys and heights of emotion

May we come to know thy self

As we die again, and again and again some more

To reveal and unveil

An exquisite raw beauty, as the light of truth.

To reflect back with fellow earth sisters,

and fellow earth brothers of many lands

Brothers and sisters of the star realms

Star-seeds, spiritual gangsters, all in-between

A time of empowering your sons and daughters

Grandsons and granddaughters yet to be birthed

Have reverence for your grandfather's and grandmothers

Send love to your fathers and mothers.

Your true nature and playful spirits are free.

We ask Mother Earth to continue to shower us

With rich offerings of abundance and colours

To be living free in peace and harmony

A place to be together for all eternity

A new Earth awaits your expansion

As the 144,000 begin to unite

As part of this ascension plan

All birthed on a prayer

Unifying Our planet,

Bathed in one love

Activated vessels of 144,000 lights

Scribed 2016.

Calling Native Indian Spirit and the Star people

Chapter 4: Raw Feminine Power

> *"The repression of the feminine has led to a planet on the edge of collapse. The re-emergence is going to be a dance to behold".*
>
> - Clare Dakin

The Power of Presence

There is an invisible power within you and felt by others. Once embodied it weaves a powerful magnet to attract that which you desire. We all have this ability, and many of us have forgotten, distracted by what others think, say or believe in. Some may unconsciously attack what is being shown, as it holds up a reflective mirror with unwavering presence. It highlights back to the observer (the one in judgment), the unseen, and this is an invitation to look deeper within. To see all beings with unconditional love and unconditional acceptance, as we are all learning how to climb out of the sand pit of the matrix and climb the ladder of growth. To continue guiding until all have ascended.

Holding presence is the ability to turn heads by walking into a room, not from how you look, but because of the magnetic glow of divine resonance around you (The Auric Field). To stand with poise and elegance whilst walking is the ability to stand-alone with confidence. Presence acts like a magnet drawing what you want to you at an accelerated rate, others will feel drawn to you, and some may wonder what the fuck is going on. This is raw feminine power and magnetic sensuality as resonance of the cosmos. Yes, consciousness and a limitless ability to create from the unmanifested.

We are a symphony of water and fire, soul and spirit, yin and yang, moon and the sun. The two energies that orchestrate the notes (expression) within this performance are the masculine and feminine energies that interweave into one.

Presence is felt when you leave a room and energy is left behind. When presence is forced due to underlying fear of rejection or abandonment it can be pushy. This creates a wave as a kick back where your presence becomes too uncomfortable for others. This may be to create a protective shield around you, or to contemplate why you are pushing others away and not seeing them as they are? Each experience is a lesson about Self and understanding boundaries. To hold presence with ease is to bring equilibrium into the space, a place where everyone has an opportunity to shift into their greatest version of self. It creates connection, mutuality and unwavering confidence with compassion. This energy to unify the space is unconditional love and unconditional acceptance. This is the ultimate path of being human.

Presence is something that some are born with, and it is observable when those are connecting with something that they are passionate about. For others, it maybe self-confidence, humility, and spiritual growth. Presence can be developed from allowing others to see into your naked soul, as in prolonged eye contact. Presence has an ease and grace and is powerful when directed by the open vulnerability of the heart and less driven by the controlling mind or the ego.

> *"A woman in harmony with her spirit is like river flowing. She goes where she will without pretence and arrives at her destination, prepared to be herself".*
> Mary Angelou

Potent presence is the ability to stand proud in who you are and to care not what others think of you. The courage to be disliked, and love Self unconditionally is the courage to be yourself. This is vital to being free to express your soul and spirit. I experienced this growing up, the nasty remarks from girls and some nasty taunts from women, yes, who I thought were friends. I laugh as it is not my stuff, and yet it is also my stuff! A test from which to grow and see them with loving compassion and chose to set boundaries in where I share my energy field and to ask what aspects I am rejecting in self to feel a reaction or trigger from the things said.

Seek solace & comfort in nature to remember who you are...

Be proud in who you are and keep inspiring others how to be free. It is refreshing to hear and feel the unspoken and to not get caught up in the distraction of it all. An opportunity to see my own 'triggers' and to forgive, walk away, send compassion and rise in love.

> *The more that people are talking about you, is a great indication you are on track. This can happen right before your life is about to upshift, as they are clouded in resentment and jealousy.*
>
> *– Zoe Bell*

Cultivating presence happens behind closed doors, with daily self-practice to work through the layers created over time. This may include overcoming suffering and adversity by implementing practices or rituals that raise your vibrational frequency. Things like physical exercise, listening to your intention, meditation and contemplation. This higher vibratory frequency is felt by a warmth within the chest area, and a lightness of being. Once you begin to access being in a state of presence, life will take on new depth and meaning. Look at a stallion as it prances around a field, free and proud. This is presence in motion. He owns his body, space and expresses elegance as a magnificent beast.

It is time to stop playing small and be willing to be seen.

There is elegance when others lash out with opinion, and the inner state remains unchangeable. There is no need to fight or react, but simply be present within stillness, to be the un-changeable state of presence. Presence is peaceful and is felt within your auric field by others.

Learn to nourish and trust in inner wisdom, to feel into when to retreat from a crowd and to be alone to attend to your resonance (auric field). No matter if you are an extrovert, feeling you need others to restore your energy, learning to fill up your cup without others is key. It is only then that you can truly shine your gifts from an authentic space. Everything comes back to Self, lessons of growth, insight gained and everyone finding their own unique way. Have non-attachment to the outcome of others, as it is time to be free of the karmic entanglements that many of you are trapped in. Especially when it comes to family. The messages and inner knowing are all in there, resting and waiting within the stillness and to be the seeker. There is no need to force presence as it will come when you let go of the need to control.

> *"The wild woman is fluent in the language of dreams, images, passion, and poetry"*
>
> – Clarissa Pinkola Estés

It is time to be free and not care what others are saying about you. Let them eat and taste their own words, smile and leave them with a trail of magical candy floss of love as you walk away. Inspire them with your joy and success, which to me is the ability to stay present within your soul truth and live with integrity. No one knows your path, better than you. Many will have an opinion of who you *should* be, but that is their opinion. Be relentless in your pursuit for presence each and every breathing moment. You are the only one who controls your vibration, so be willing to *un-ravel yourself* from an individual or societal opinion. Society may still reject you as you threaten the lies that are being taught.

SELF-CONFIDENCE - INNER RADIANCE

Self-confidence is Your radiance. Saying exactly what you desire is sizzling hot, and men and women love it. No one likes second-guessing what you are thinking. It is easier to look deeper within when we are feeling good, and these will give you ways to begin to feel super empowered and kick-ass sexy amazing.

Say it as it is – The way you choose to express will be fluid and interchangeable to suit the mood and situation. At times it may be softer with your feminine essence to flow through. This at times may be mixed dirty talk. You can be direct in a classy and sensual way. I've heard from men that talking crude is a big turn off. Never be afraid to say what you desire and how you feel, open up into your raw vulnerability. This is a huge hurdle to step over for many and, yet on the other side of fear is love, acceptance and a magical beginning.

- How can you be more present?
- Be willing to express the real you in each raw moment?
- Do you recognise when you feel flat in your emotions?
- Are you taking action or getting stuck complaining?
- Are you honouring each emotion as a valuable messenger?
- Is there a part of you that you don't like?
- Are you critical of others, or more about Self?
- Are there emotions you ignore?
- Can you shift your feeling state, whenever you choose?

Care less if others like you, listen to your heart, and honour the messages, as this is the only real truth. Find your Tribe and honour your Vibe until you have the courage to step away from the tribe and explore your own way which may require going a little off track.

WILDFLOWER

Wild free spirit of the Moon

I've seen you before

In the depths of my dreams

Your words unspoken

Deep within my soul

An insatiable passion

Cracks me open wide

The glowing moon tickles in passion

Moon spirit leaps into expansion

Layers upon layer

Melting away

Rebirthing unique gifts

Into a new day.

An intoxicating emotion

A passionate potion

Diverse - sacred momentum

Once untethered & unleashed

There is no breaking this force

Sacred spirit, awakening of course

RAW FEMININE POWER

Infused into ecstasy

Intoxicating passion

Of sweet love, mysticism

Peace & harmony golden chrism

The lady of the moon

Fearless and free

Oozing deep sensuality

Seductive vulnerability

No holding back

Her gifts now awakened

Unleashed and unpacked

Alive and awakened

Born to be free

Wild free spirit is her Earth name

Never to be contained

Or maimed again!

Your attempts to control

Will be laughed at in vain

WILDFLOWER

As she throws her head back

Confidently tossing back her mane

As her courageous soul is set free

Can never be tamed or suppressed again.

Dance within and without her presence

As her magnetic allure draws you in,

Be swept up by her magnetic potion

A Sensual allure – all to explore

To find your own flow

To be free for ever more

Within this scared dance

Rests the great spirits, deep romance.

Stand tall empowered by your truth

Taste into her sweetness of freedom within

Her hypnotic trance of love and divinity

Within and without

Under this full moon

A magnetic motion of pulsating bodies

Captivating, illuminating

Deliciously intoxicating

Savoring each sweet breath

Drinking up a love of pure ecstasy

As you dive in deeper & deeper

Exploring one another's pleasure

The sacred dance builds

Within one another

One sacred pulse of moon Spirit love.

Chapter 5: Touch for Human Survival

"That's what it feels like when you touch me. Like millions of tiny universes being born and then dying in the space between your finger and my skin. Sometimes I forget." - Iain Thomas

Touch and Development

Touch is the greatest sensation within the body and is vital for the survival of our human species. There was a study on children from orphanages in Romania, many of you may have already heard of it, it was a famous study called *Failure to thrive*. It addresses how human touch is more vital for healthy nourishment and human development than food.

By definition: Failure to thrive is when the efforts of a living being to continue to live, internally or externally, ultimately cease. This state of condition is seen among infants and children who were orphaned and abandoned.

Each and every one of you will have received some form of traumatic event in your life. It is feelings around these events in these early years (rejection, abandonment, loss of a loved one, beginning your periods, rape, sexual abuse and accidents and other events related to connection with your environment and body.) These events are having a direct cause to why opening up in intimacy is challenging. Unresolved trauma, and bound emotions remain in the tissues of the mind and body. It is a key to creating healthy intimate relationships with Self and learning how to relate with others. With the events of 2020 and into 2021 and to so called 'Pandemic' touch was denied to loved ones transitioning through the dying process and those in sickness. Touch is healing as it releases many pain-relieving substances and provides comfort through being in compassion. Suicide cases increased and more experienced isolation which was over-whelming on the psyche for those that had never learnt the tools of even implemented ways to nourish the soul beyond external gratification of desires and social conditioning of the group. I did not feel any loss of touch as breathing with awareness was being touched by the holy spirit of the goddess Source within. I felt connected to the great spirit of nature as isolation is a magical time for personal spiritual development. It was a time to nourish alongside my teenage boys and connect through laughter, conversations and massaging one another, as they experienced isolation for the first time. In saying this, they were encouraged to go outside on their bikes and play with friends.

Womb work is done one to one, guiding both Men and Women through a 21- day rebirthing. (As you will later discover men have a spiritual womb). This healing pathway begins to remember the light in the tissues and awaken the cosmic juices, known as *amrit*. A pathway to fully open into your sensual wholeness as a feminine goddess. A woman does not need a man to penetrate her, she requires a man to hold space as he is vital to reach higher states together. She is the key to open up into worlds that can only be experienced. She needs a man's heart devotion to her, that she trusts as she devotes her heart to him. An awakened woman requires a man to be doing the deep inner work on Self as together they reach states of cosmic orgasmic bliss. Before this happens, there is healing to do done by each individual, as this feminine essence of light is to be seen in the beauty she was so magically created by God. This is healing, lifegiving and a path to sacred sensuality and states of bliss consciousness.

Let's glance at the energy wheels, known as chakras, and how they relate to healthy development. This is from my own personal journey of working with great teachers and exploring in my own space. It is an honour to share and pass on this womb wisdom on within the healing space and is linked to awakening the dormant kundalini lifeforce energy which is curled up as the serpent at the base of the spine. This is a key to raising consciousness and exploring the true wisdom of sacred sensuality either alone or with your beloved. There is no hiding from the inner womb healing as the light will shine upon what is hidden. For many the pelvis is locked in the sacrum region, and this impedes the natural sensual flow.

- 0-7 - 1st Chakra – Root – feeling safe, grounded and connected
- 8-14 - 2nd Chakra – Sacral – creativity and sensual expression
- 15-21 - 3rd Chakra – Solar plexus – identity to self and confidence
- 22-29 - 4th Chakra – Heart – ability to give and receive love and forgive
- 30-37 - 5th Chakra – Throat – clear expression – speaking your truth
- 38-44 - 6th Chakra – Third Eye – clear seeing – into the unknown
- 45- 52 - 7th Chakra – Bliss State – higher states of consciousness

The first 7-years are the foundation of stability to feel safe, grounded and connected. To belong to a family and tribe and it is vital to our survival as a species. The next 7-year cycle is where sensuality and sensual exploration and creativity reveal, then the next 7-year cycle, and the 'who and I, sense of self.' The point I wish to express is many remain looping in a crazy-8 caught up in old karmic patterns in the early years of development and this can be rewired, resolved and risen from no matter how messed up you think you are! There are many distortions playing out in society as patterns of survival to keep you stuck in your own suffering. Take hiding in groups of causes for example with an expectation to be validated by others. This is the socialized mind, the faithful follower, the team player and reliance on the group to survive and staying bound in obedience that feeds the story and afraid to see what is beyond the fence.

You have read my story and even with all the breakthroughs, there was still more inner work of self-discovery and womb healing to be done. I was late in exploring womb healing as my arrogance got in the way, thinking I had my shit together. As mentioned earlier, it was in September 2020, that I reached out and began another step and visited the entire back story in the session. My ego was, I have gone over this many times and I laugh looking back as there were aspects of arrogance and shame still hiding. It was a divine masculine that called out my masculine protective armour and there was no hiding. As I took myself through the 21-days I began to experience the greater light and began to radiate this through my sensitive vulva tissues. I was guided through self-healing and the raw emotions released. My entire vulva shifted in her expression and what was imbalanced began to radiate glowing light and I felt joy for the first time in my life. Since, I have guided many women how to restore the light to their yoni tissues. This is a vital step in stirring the sacred feminine life-giving waters of the sacrum.

For all reading this the path is to step away from the group and become the self-authority of your mind and being the leader of self. To navigate this transition in development requires a compass, a map and to be independent in problem solving. This is why this healing is supported by a mentor and the restoring of the tissues is guided to be performed by the individual. The path is a dance between the student and teacher of Self. Life is a beautiful journey where each pivotal inner shift restores fluidly with natural alignment of healthy development. May this inspire you to keep unravelling and exploring. It is reason why re-releasing the first birthing (book1), required re-writing. I am no longer the story sharing in a state of chaos and I celebrate the innocence and beauty of the path of sensual freedom I was remembering with its many faces. My past, a blank slate, with no attachment to any of it. This is true peace and freedom.

In next chapter 6, *Restoring Healthy Sensuality through Healing Rituals* guides ways to begin to release the tension held in the tissues of the genitals.

Touch is greater nourishment for the soul than food! 2020 and 2021 was an experience of many not being hugged for days, weeks or months as they had no physical contact with others. I saw this is a transition to exploring the 'inner healing work' to reconnect to self. Needing touch from another all the time may be stemming from a place of lack within Self. It is vital to nourish Self rather than an expectation of another to do it for you. All expectations lead to inevitable disappointment and suffering. Touch affects their emotional, spiritual, psychological and physical wellbeing. Touch is healing for the *mind, body and Spirit.*

My beautiful family and wise teachers that keep it real...

The Benefits of Touch

Physical level:

Endorphins are released = Happiness

Touch makes You feel loved. I invite you to explore different sensations of touch with light touching and perhaps brushing the skin. Enquire which you enjoy as maybe there are some you have never explored. Touch yourself every day in the shower all over, sending love, gratitude and appreciation for all that you are.

Emotional Level:

Letting Go and Receiving Love.

Allowing another to touch and love your body is one of the most beautiful experiences ever, it is freedom. Touch is felt through words, music and poetry, as they reach deep into your soul. Touch another with your words and the unique song you express from your heart. Being held and gently touched at the vulnerable places upon the body by fellow goddesses or godliness with permission is healing.

Here is a permission sequence to voice.

- Is it safe and okay to touch?
- How would you like to be touched?
- Would you prefer soft or firm strokes?

Keep the *line of communication open* so you always feel safe and in that are able to let go and open with freedom to express touch or no touch, all responses are welcomed.

Psychological Level:

It Feels Good & Soothing.

Anything that feels good and brings no harm to others is going to benefit your psyche right! As You develop in utero, your hands grow out of our heart at around week 7/40. In essence when you give hugs you are wrapping your heart around the other. Hugs can feel really good or drain on your energy. Choose who you hug and own your No. Never reject a child that needs to be hugged or a friend in need in a time of pain.

Spiritual Level:

Touch reaches deep into the Soul.

Your natural essence and life force energies are sensual in nature. You are each energetic beings with a natural tendency to touch, be touched and be close to one another. The breath is a direct way to experience the potent life-force of you and the Yoni-verse.

Cuddling feels good: Did you know that there is scientific research to back up, that cuddling makes you feel really good? Cuddling releases *Oxytocin, The Love Hormone,* and it makes us feel good and connected to others. When you cuddle another, oxytocin is released. This is also the hormone that is released following orgasm. Cuddling and kissing boosts the immune system.

Hugging relieves pain: The oxytocin released will reduce the pain experienced; you will be less focused on the pain, as you will feel loved up. Even the touch of your own hands will relieve pain in the body. Touch more and self soothe the body, go out and hug someone today.

Toning gets you connected with your body: Touch your body all over, after a shower. This is a daily ritual of self-love by toning the skin. Embark upon self-nourishment of the soul by assisting the circulatory system to wake-up, cultivating firmer skin and restore tone.

Dry- Toning of The Body

Tune into the sensations of the body as this is a stimulating practice and like you are needing dough, almost with a strong pinching touch.

- Start with either foot
- Work up the calf – knee- thigh to groin
- Repeat on the other side
- Belly- but-waist
- Chest- arm pits – shoulders -arms- hands
- Back- neck-head-face

Tune into the sensations, be still and feel the awakened sensation.

SHIFTING FROM NUMBNESS TO SENSATION

You may feel some numbness to the fullness of life, perhaps, dulled from the foods you eat, your environment and maybe more time on the internet rather than connecting with passions. Perhaps, in your relationship You are *touch deprived* or worse feel uncomfortable with masturbation, which I will refer to as self-pleasure. Your skin is a doorway that holds residual tension of emotions and trauma held hostage in the tissues. Perhaps, you use self-pleasure to feel better, or to get to sleep at night. Are you addicted to a sex toy and even your Yoni egg and have become codependent on it to feel something? If this is so, perhaps there is a level of disconnection and numbness in your body, blocking pure sensuality to flow freely and to experience sensuality beyond objectivity.

Explore these questions and ask yourself: (take notes in a journal)

- Do you know how to trust your yes, and no?
- Are you able to express with confidence?
- Are you able to relax and receive?
- Do you feel worthy to receive?
- Do you perform, in fear of him or her leaving?
- Have you denied yourself the space to let go?
- Are you able to totally surrender?
- What are you most afraid of?

It is my intention throughout this book to open up a safe and loving conversation with your most vulnerable and intimate aspects. If you are feeling some numbness and desensitisation when it comes to self-pleasuring, then I invite you leap past 'exploring masturbation' and begin with the healing rituals in the Chapter 6. You can revisit sections of the book whenever you feel ready!

Touching your body for self-pleasure is natural and healthy

Exploring Masturbation

Your body is a pleasurable temple and masturbation feels good. Masturbation is safe and healthy in your comfortable privacy. Sensual pleasure is free of guilt to discover what you like and enjoy with sensuous body responses. *Guiltless masturbation is the cornerstone of successful sex education* and yield major life-long benefits, especially for females. It is not about the orgasm and many have become numb from using plastic and mechanical devices such as vibrators. This is adding to the disconnection and numbness of the sensual body and many are depleted on the healing sensual life force energy as they are leaking it all in orgasms.

- Do you recall masturbating as a child/teenager?
- Did you ever feel guilty about your secret pleasure?
- Do you masturbate?
- Do you feel guilty masturbating without your partner?
- Is it a dirty little secret?
- Do you have to use porn to climax?

Masturbation to porn and excessive masturbating many times a day depletes your energy and there are ways to cycle and loop the sensual life-giving energy before the orgasm happens. The pleasure sensation is a doorway to accessing higher states of consciousness rather that leaking all the energy and shifting the body into acidity. These practices are shared in Soul Codes.

In society, many are stuck at the lower energy centers, and are depleting their lifeforce energy with masturbation, sex and blocks in healthy human development. If you look tired around the eyes and drawn in the face then you are depleted and are running on empty. A sign of an imbalance in the root and sacral chakra (1st & 2nd energy centre). This can be reversed and rebalanced with womb & yoni energy healing. Let's continue this sensuality journey in the next chapter.

Chapter 6: Healthy Sensuality & Healing Rituals

"It's the one in the mirror that was the enemy. The same one that beats me up, who made up the monsters and who stripped me of my dignity and confidence. I see you and now I'm going to love every aspect of you unconditionally!" – Zoe-Anna

Sexuality and Sensuality

Before we explore different healing rituals it is vital to address the distinction between sexuality and sensuality. Based on life experiences, personally and professionally I'll endeavour to explain the differences.

Sexuality is based on identification to form. Such as gender differences, the labels you call yourself to tell others what your sexual preferences are. This is based on societies social and possibly pop culture trends, to what you think or feel you fit into. This creates a sense of belonging into the specific sexually orientated group of that identification based on attachment to identity.

The term sexual, is the primal attraction towards another individual and the feeling state of sexual arousal, felt in the genitals, the dilatation of the pupils, and the nervous system preparing for sexual connection, as in mating. It is an immediate response with a physical reaction, where the desires and lust to connect may be overwhelming. *I see it as the instant X Factor that you see and feel in another.*

The term sensual is an energetic feeling state that is present within the entire body 24/7. This feeling state is easily felt in relaxation and when the mind is relaxed as in first rising in the morning. This omnipresent energetic resonance that is our natural state of being. It is the lifeforce energy that flows through us and emits our radiance seen within our auric field. It is the harmonic connection between souls as in affection, unconditional love, kindness and compassion. It has an ease and effortless grace to it and is the healing power of the universe and cosmos. Everything in life becomes a sensual dance of exploration and joy. It is both the light and the darkness.

Sensuality is wild, free and creative expression and it has been misused by abuse of its pure lifeforce energy and marketed as sex, to feed off its pure light and magical essence. Much of societies intimacy has been lost due to acts of sex where unaddressed and un-healed shame, blame, guilt and trauma remain in the psyche, and the tissues from past events. It is my pure intention that these self-love rituals will play a role in restoring healthy sensuality and begin a path to restoring innocence through healing self-touch and sensual play. It is key in evolution of the future human and free from demonic forces.

HEALTHY SENSUALITY & HEALING RITUALS

Sensuality is invisible and formless – it is free and graceful

Sensuality is within all vortexes of energy 1st -13th Chakras.

Sexuality is identity and seeks attention – for recognition, power and control

Sexuality is from the 1st energy centre (root) to the solar plexus, 3rd energy vortex.

We need both sexuality and sensuality. It is the inner child wound held within the body, the unhealed sexual programming and the stuck emotions all require acknowledging, embracing and healing. You have a choice how you choose to show up life and it is a moment-to-moment choice. To remind you that this is a path to reclaim innocence and shift the wounded child into the awakened child. The path of the Divine union of the Mother – Father and the golden child. There is no hiding from the truth of your own mirror, as what others choose to do, is really none of your business. This is your life to access your divinity and bring that divinity of pure love into action.

> *"Sexuality and sensuality are completely different things. Sensuality is something that you're born with. But sexuality is something that I leave for my own mirror."* - Ricky Martin

BREATHING AND TRUSTING IN LETTING GO

It is your breath that connects you with the field of consciousness as a sensual and omnipresent elixir lifeforce. It is the weaving of the electromagnetic being that you are in all your sensual wholeness, in divine expression. It cleverly orchestrates events that are magnetically drawn to you for life lessons to gain the teaching and have the direct experience. Your breath is consciousness learning about itself, in this human form called a mind-body vessel and the experience of being human and becoming closer to God.

Letting go, is what most fear and the breath is a doorway to leaning into deeper trust and faith in what is not known. Your breath is the first thing you instinctively do when you enter this world, and the last thing you do as you leave this physical form.

As Esther Hicks the voice of Abraham" so eloquently expressed, 'You croak it at the death experience.' I love this raw and blunt explanation, as you like me are simply energy and this death transition energy is changing form. Energy and Spirit cannot die, and each end (death) is another beginning (birth), as you are an infinite being. As you venture along your spiritual path you will have many death experiences. Yes, many *dark nights of the soul* as rising out of the ashes as the phoenix is not one single event! It will be however many times is requiring all to get out the way of the false self (ego). You have to learn how to unravel yourself LAYA by layer and not mistaking your ego (small self) for your Highest Self, the ego for the soul. This is known as 'AVIDYA', a Sanskrit term for 'not knowing.'

Think of the breath as a seductive exhale and an invitation to let go and be present in the now. Life is a moment-to-moment happening, constantly changing to align for Your greatest growth. The Mastery of letting go is the greatest lesson to learn in this human experience along with heartbreak as letting go opens the heart to infinite pure love. Sounds so easy, right?!

Meditation and the ease of letting go

"The heart surrenders to everything to the moment. The mind judges and holds back"

Ram Dass

WHAT ARE YOU HOLDING ONTO?

- Attachments to places, objects, beliefs and people
- Your story
- Your opinion
- Circumstances
- Drama
- A relationship
- A boring job
- An old way of behaving or being
- Attachment to pain and suffering

Holding on to what was feeds inner suffering and is tainted in fear, and it is the shadow of control. Letting go requires trust, faith and a willingness learn what you don't know. It is the state of allowing all that is to be as it is, without the need to fix or change it. You naturally let go in many ways.

- Crying
- Orgasming
- Breathing out.
- Moaning
- Laughing
- Sighing
- Screaming
- Shouting
- Farting

- Quaffing
- Blogging and writing
- Dancing
- Sneezing
- Purging
- Shaking
- Defecating
- Dying 'Croaking experience'
- And the simplest of all, giving letting go a go!

They are all ways to release energy, which is letting go.

Sometimes, life persuades You to let go, even if that is being dragged by your heels kicking and screaming. The breath restores equilibrium, presence, connection and clarity. You can learn to control and manipulate the breath(lifeforce) through a practice known as pranayama.

Pranayama is the regulation and conscious awareness of the breath through techniques and practices. The first word is composed of two Sanskrit words. The first part of the word Prana means life-force, and 'Yama' means the restrain or control of the prana or lifeforce. The 'Ayama' translates to expansion of this life-force. This has many benefits on the nervous system, endocrine system, success, abundance, disease, sexual magnetism and mental wellbeing.

The N.S Arousal Response in the Body

Sympathetic:

As You breathe in the sympathetic nervous system is activated thus energising and activating your state of being. When the body remains in a heightened state of the sympathetic nervous system arousal as in flight or fight, your natural sensual response and connection will diminish.

Parasympathetic:

As You breathe out the parasympathetic nervous system is activated bringing about relaxation and a calm state of being. Relaxation is the optimum state of arousal for intimate connection, healthy sensual responses and love.

When an individual is in a state of freeze, the body has been in a prolonged sympathetic nervous system arousal with no reset. This debilitating state translates to the body shutting down as in dissociation, disconnection and numbness. This is seen in withdrawal from the environment and people in your life. It is the nervous system's preparation for death. Many are still living in this state and these healing rituals will assist. My details are at the back of the book and often require working one to one and receive support and pure loving guidance.

It is important NOT to confuse disconnection with retreating inwards to exploring inner work and honouring seclusion. Saying no to others that you no longer choose to share your lifeforce with is healthy. Know how and when to draw the line in the sand, own your life.

Breathing Awareness Rituals

Begin to breathe with awareness whilst sitting in stillness. With each inhalation and exhalation begin the notice the gentle rise and fall of the chest. There is nothing to control or change, simply notice and become aware of the observation of your breathing. Relaxed breathing of a smooth inhalation and a long exhalation. With each exhale notice a relaxed feeling state and repeat the word relax, as you do this consciously invite your shoulders, mouth and face to relax and soften. Do this as many times a day as you like, as consistency with awareness is the key.

This breathing exercise will allow you to see how You are connected with the universe. You may like to record this dialogue with your voice to play back before you close your eyes. Give it and go monitor this breathing exercise for 5 minutes. This is a doorway to remember your natural state of peace.

You-niverse Breath

- Sit and softly close your eyes
- Notice your breath as it moves in and out
- Now as you breathe out, imagine the universe breathing in
- As you breathe in, imagine the universe is breathing out
- You are at one within the universe
- Feeling held and safe by the universe
- You are never alone.
- Feel her pulse within and without you
- Enjoy this dancing of your energy of that the universe, as one.

- Explore the dancing of your energy in your body and then with another
- With this simple remembrance, we can access a way to be present.
- Observe the pause between your inhale and exhale, notice your own resonance expand.

Awareness requires integration of practices or rituals to assist personal growth.

The process of learning how to breathe with awareness at first is a state of conscious incompetence. Over time, with practice this will progress into conscious competence and then finally it will become second nature in unconscious competence. This will bring you into a deeper resonance and present state of consciousness. You may find that certain words written in the book activate you, as I am guided by Source.

Breathing is a doorway into many realms, and it is the sensual thread that weaves us all together, like a silky golden thread. It was within my own self-directed practices of breathing exploration that I experienced the 'void', an infinite space of nothingness and profound peace. It cannot be described as it is formless. The Absolute, zero point and completion from where we all return back to.

It cannot be found; it presents when you stop seeking it.

Before you dive into the rituals and intimacy exercises, have a read through to invite a clear way of seeing and loving you. Be guided how you feel and see which resonates with you. I would highly recommend starting at the beginning with the 'I love you' as the eyes are the windows to your soul. When you start there, then the other ones will be smoother. There is no rush with this, and it is vital to spend time on one at a time. Be gentle as there is no rush. The body will let go only when it is ready, there is no force. Having said that, you have to be willing to go to your edge! And into an area that feels uncomfortable.

Change will never happen unless You learn to play at the edge!

MIRROR WORK - I LOVE YOU

It is time to rise in love with your soul and the deep hidden aspects of You. As you begin to open with this ritual over time the eyes of judgment will lessen, and it will become easier to be seen by another. An intimate doorway to unveil your Soul. You will need a mirror as you explore this ritual, be aware to keep breathing as belly deep as you can. As when we face what is uncomfortable and scary the breath becomes shallow, so in the upper chest. Like many of these rituals you may want to record your voice to do this without being distracted by the book.

- Stand in front of a mirror.
- Gaze softly into your eyes.
- Pause and become aware of your breathing
- Allowing your gaze to be still and just be
- Try not to look away - begin to see beyond the eyes
- Meet your soul deep within your eyes
- Gaze courageously into your eyes.

- Try to not look away, it is safe to be here
- This is the doorway into your sacred space
- The meaning of *In-to-me-see*
- Gaze deep into your soul
- *In-to-me-see* and allow each emotion to arise
- Allow tears to bubble up, you are safe, and never alone
- I am soul, in here you will find me.
- I am love and I am courage
- I never left you
- I am here
- I am love
- I am eternal
- Welcome home.

This is a transformational ritual opening up your ability to form deeper and more intimate connections. Keep gazing and releasing with loving kindness. Embrace the perceived shame, the uninvited blame and invite them all in to be loved. Know that You are safe, you are loved, and you are enough. Look deeper within and try not to look away.

Yes, you may cry, that is okay

You may sob deeply crying a river

It is okay to not be okay

Yes, you may shake, and that is okay

HEALTHY SENSUALITY & HEALING RITUALS

You may want to run, and I invite you to stay.

You may want to hide, and I invite you to play

I welcome you back, and perhaps you laugh

At each uncomfortable emotion, I have your back,

Allow the tears to flow, to welcome your smile

Repeat after me.

I love you- hold your gaze- I love you- its' you and you.

REPEAT as many times as you need and hold your gaze.

Say hello to your Soul. Tell her or him how much you are here to dance a new dance together, side by side and never to be feel alone again.

You are sensual and you are safe,

Deliciously juicy and playfully fun

I choose you, yes, the beautiful reflection of you

I meet you in the mirror and we rise together in love.

Run a relaxing bath or warm shower and continue to rest into you with soothing music whilst sipping a warm drink, it is vital to allow each emotion to be honoured with gentle integration.

Body Love Through Movement

Let's explore movement and touching to awaken the sensual body with loving acceptance. It takes a second to think a negative thought, and thirty seconds to create a new belief.

It is time to connected in love with your beautiful body, as the dancer of your own life.

You may want to read through this first and then allow your intuition to guide you, or perhaps to record these words and then be guided by your own voice. See which you resonate with.

Choose music you love, set the scene with candles and begin to move your body slowly. Make small circles with the hips and let go of any thoughts, begin to stretch your arms above your head, out to the sides and really begin to own your sacred space. As you move, feel into the sensations of your body and when ready begin to lightly touch your fingers over your body. Touch your neck, face, with light touches and smile into this self-honouring. Avoid the breasts and all other aspects that are associated with being seen as sexual. You are inviting sensuality back into your body remembrance.

Begin to trace the lines down your arms, the creases of the elbow and around the wrist, even drawing circles in the palms of your hands, change hands and notice any changes in sensations in your body. Enjoy the shivers that rush through the skin and through every cell of your body.

Move your body to the music as if no one is watching and no one is judging. If you feel self-conscious keep moving and firmly tell the inner critic to *be quiet and sit the fu3k down!* This is your party and negative comments are not invited. Get your sensual groove on baby.

Run your hands across your shoulders, your upper back, lower back around your waist from your arm pits to your hips and move at your pace and keep breathing; feeling the pleasure increasing in the body, as you start to touch your body all over. Stay here for as long as you desire.

When you feel connected to your sensual body begin to run your fingers lightly across your nipples, breasts tracing slowly down to your waist, lightly brushing across your yoni or lingam. Explore here for a while, slow long strokes all over the body, feeling the sensations awakening in your skin. There is no need to rush and all to explore the sensation of each moment. Allow the sensual energy to build up, explore and become curious to a different conversation and connection with your body, away from over-sexualisation and performing.

Keep moving your hands, dancing slowly and allow everything to relax. The physical layers of the body soften with your touch your energetic body awakening. Become aware of your breath as a sensual thread opening you into a deep connection with Self. Stand still and allow the full sensations of lifeforce to intensify, the divine expression of who you are bathed in life. Allowing whatever to arise to arise, as your breath is free and effortless with your belly totally relaxed and a soft warm smile splashes across your face. Gaze lovingly into the mirror and see the beauty before you. Honour your strong body, hearts courage and warm hug of embodied wholeness.

You are enough.

Claim your sovereignty, a Queen and Empowered Goddess of Kunta, a Sacred Flower

Body Work for Yoni Healing

Yoni-verse Breath

Begin to breathe with awareness in stillness and with each inhalation and exhalation begin the notice the gentle rise and fall of your belly. There is nothing to control or change, simply notice and become aware of the observation of your breathing in and out of your belly. Relaxed breathing of a smooth inhalation and a long exhalation. With each exhale notice a relaxed feeling state and repeat the word relax, as you do this consciously invite your hips, thighs, pelvis, and face to relax and soften. Do this as many times a day as you like, as consistency with awareness is the key. Bring the heels up towards the bottom and feet together, allow the knees to drop open and out to the side. Perhaps, for comfort place two rolled towels under the outside of your knees.

This breathing exercise will allow you to connect with Your Yoni-verse. You may like to record this dialogue with your voice to play back before you close your eyes. Try to monitor this breathing exercise for 5 minutes.

Once the belly is relaxed bring the awareness lower into the genitals and begin to breathe in and out of your yoni. Imagine there is a straw in your vagina, and as you draw the breath in, draw gently upwards like gently sucking fluid up the straw and then as you exhale, fully relax the muscles in the vagina and release. Monitor this breathing exercise for 5 minutes.

- Sit and softly close your eyes
- Notice your breathing in and out, relaxed breathing.
- As you inhale, draw up like drinking fluid up a straw
- The exhale, relax and let go of the vaginal muscles
- Keep breathing in this way, as if your vagina is a straw
- See your yoni as connected to the universe
- Stay here, and feel into the wholeness of your yoni
- Feel into the vastness of the universe
- Now imagine as your breathing out, the universe is breathing in
- As you breathe in, the universe is breathing out
- You are one, penetrated by the universe
- Welcome to your *Yoni of the universe*
- It is simple and with awareness, anyone can do this.
- The letting go and release is vital for deep relaxation.

Breathing in this way will deepen your intimate connection with your sensual life-force energy. Even imagine a jelly fish and how jelly fish move through water, drawing up and in and gently letting go in a very sensual flowing pulse. The men can do this by imagining breathing in and out of the perineum- the area between the scrotum and the anus. When this area is activated, the penis will lift up and down. Once you start to tap into it, you don't want to rush the deliciousness of it. Enjoy the opening and expansive feeling, as once you taste its sweetness you want to explore it. The only thing you have to learn to do is let go of the need to control and simply be within your own space. When you are ready you may wish to explore the state of connectedness within another's space. This awakens energy deep inside your yoni and sacral area. This is also the doorway for men to activate themselves from the root and sacral energy centre.

WILDFLOWER

This assists with feeling into the connectedness of everything around you, and the beginning of learning how to work with this energy and remembrance of Self as an electromagnetic being of energy, water and fire. The essence of the Goddess Source as the Holy Spirit. Explore all the Chakra activation points with your Yoni and his Lingam with loving awareness and begin to inner stand intimacy, relationships and how loving connection is required to open the heart.

If you are single, then the next diagram will explain how one-night stands can leave you feeling depleted and damages your heart over time that is longing for love. Be honest and real and enjoy your personal reflexology journey.

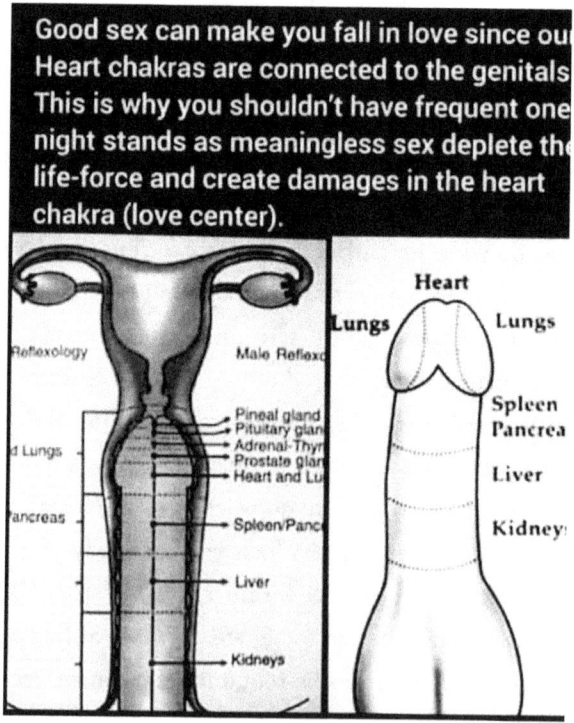

Flowering Lotus

This is a way to begin to explore the tension held bound in the delicate tissues of the genitals, the Pubis Mondi's, groin, labial outer lips and the testes of men. Allow this to be a self-discovery to notice specific areas of pain and discomfort. This is a doorway for sensual healing and a step that I explore one to one in womb healing for both men and women.

Find a sacred place like your bed to practice this. Using your first two fingers and your thumb begin with the skin and flesh that protects the pubic bone. Begin gently by pinching the flesh between these two fingers and thumb to then releasing. As you pinch gently begin to roll the flesh as you may hear and feel creaking under the skin, almost like a bubble wrap popping. Welcome to stored emotions, and layers of tension in the body. Become the explorer and see what comes up for You. Massage like this for around 3 mins and then be still and notice any changing in energy flowing down the thighs, repeat and see what you notice.

Next explore the tissues surrounding and of the outer labia for women and for men the testes. Massaging, gently squeezing and feeling into the tension under the skin. Go into the tension and this shift into a deeper massage, so breath into it. This is not about rushing into self-pleasuring as this will keep you bound in the sexual focus of the genitals. This bodywork Self massage with begin to awaken the delicate tissues that assist with blood flow and lifeforce into the divine sensual vessel of You. There is way too much attention placed on the lingam shaft and the clitoral head in many massages and the clitoral organ runs deep into the body. See the picture below. I repeat, chasing the orgasm will keep you bound in old patterns of sexual conditioning and performance. My intention is to invite and share a deeper healing in sensuality and allow lifeforce energy to shift beyond the genitals into whole body pleasure.

NOT MUCH DIFFERENCE

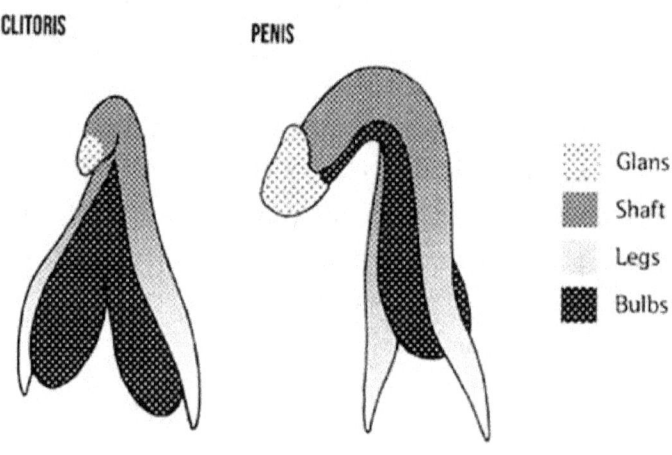

YONI LOVE FLOWERING RITUAL

This next piece is here to inspire You how to love your yoni. Your sacred doorway into of all creation, a sweet nectar of joyous lifeforce of warm wisdom.

Your yoni is a beautiful flower, that You get to open, and you get to invite in, as you choose. I am your guide to open a realm how to express your truth, in how you like to be touched, caressed and held in all your sensual unapologetic wholeness. It is time to see your beauty in all her glory and heal any shame, self-judgment or self-loathing. This can be scary, as it is deeply healing and every morning since 2011, I have practiced this Yoni-love ritual.

Holy f*ck, initially this may be the scariest thing, especially if you have never made time in your day to fully explore your most powerful and sacred temple. Mirror work is super powerful, and this is my yoni ritual of my day. It has been sad to hear men say this picture is hot and sexy rather than the vulnerability of the feminine and profound healing being revealed. Get comfortable doing this alone as it is time to stop being seen as sexual visual to arouse another. This is not porn and not to get your partner off.

- Find a mirror that can rest on the floor, be comfortable & naked
- Connect with Self, look into your eyes
- Hey, how are you beautiful Soul?
- Connect with your breath and look into your eyes.
- Begin to slowly open your thighs
- Connect with the yoni-verse breathing
- Gaze lovingly at your beautiful flower
- Gaze adoringly and smile at her uniqueness
- Full acceptance and full honour
- Full adoration of her unique beauty
- Feel love & peace within all your being
- You are beautiful as a precious rose
- Gaze at her flowering beauty
- Allowing her blossoming magic to unfold

Yoni love flowering ritual

Deeper Healing

- Say, I am sorry I dishonoured your beauty
- Hold her whole uniqueness, Your mystical flower
- You are powerful and beautiful
- I love you and I accept all of my flesh
- I love you and I am sorry for dishonouring You
- I deserve to experience pleasure
- I deserve to feel beautiful
- Place the left hand over your yoni and hold
- Place your right hand over your heart

- Be still and breathe love and acceptance
- I am complete in my womanliness
- I embrace all aspect of me NOW.
- I honour my uniqueness
- I honour my love, I own my voice
- I own my choices, empowered to say No
- Empowered to say Yes.
- You are mysterious and divine
- The wonder of the universe
- My own joy and my pleasure
- To share and do as I choose
- My sweet ocean of bliss…
- My Yoni-verse.

Your body is a beautiful container of love and pleasure abounds you. Enjoy the journey back to you. You can do this alone of when you feel ready with your partner and send love and talk lovingly to your beautiful flower. Remember, you have to establish boundaries of self-love, so others can begin to treat you differently. This is great practice for men to begin to explore the true beauty of the yoni and to apologise for all the times he fed off her essence, dishonouring her wisdom and is a vital step of men growing into adulthood.

Connect to be guided in this *transformational womb healing* and addressing the inner programs held in the tissues from when you navigated those sacred 7-year cycles of development as a sensual being. This is the p*ath to embody higher vibrational light and access cosmic bliss.*

Below is a taste of what will be explored in Soul Codes, and from the section, 'A Potent Jewel within'. This will intensify sensual activations and plays a role in raising consciousness. This ancient practice has a direct impact on sensual tone of the vagina and restores inner calm and peace. I stopped all Kegel exercises as soon as I learnt this way, and over the years self-mastery to it be a psychic activation, meaning as soon as I have awareness, my yoni and whole body are in full sensual activation. I never had to use a Yoni egg as I learnt how to activate from within. As this is an aspect of your yoni healing journey, it is important to firstly address the emotions, tension and bound flow in the tissues before adding more lifeforce into your sacred vessel and getting trapped in another method and chasing pleasure in the genitals lost in a fleeting localised orgasm, this is explored in Soul Codes.

A Potent Jewel Within

There is a place within that once you can access it will restore your energy, stir and awaken the Kundalini life-force energy and raise your consciousness, whilst being in a very calm, connected and centred place. Within the body there are three bandhas which are dormant, in the body, they are situated in the throat, abdomen and perineum.

A Correlation Between the Throat and Yoni

Perhaps, your voice is shut down and you get spoken over by others. This build up the inner rage and anger which gets pushed down, all to stay small and blend in, all to be invisible? Your voice is a gift and learning how to speak so others listen is often mastered through observing others. Learn to absorb wisdom and integrate so when you do speak, others listen are lining up to listen. Moaning is a great way for learning to let go and unleashing your sensual prowess. It is time to let go of pretending to moan during lovemaking which has turned into a performance like a porn star or faking your climax to get it over with. It is your human right to be free, open and unapologetic in expression. Is your pelvic floor constantly held in tension and contraction? If you said yes, then I bet your voice is feeling shut down as the pelvic floor is like trap door held shut.

Sound familiar? You are not alone, and this is why awareness is the light of truth to set you free! It is super delicious to roar and growl when you orgasm where nothing is held back and no care to how you sound or look. It is powerful to speak without having to think as the words flow from your shameless heart and soul.

OPEN UP AND MOAN

There is a direct relationship with moaning and climaxing through orgasm.

- Sound moaning

Ancient Taoist sexology say that your throat is connected to your yoni. When your throat is opened to sound your yoni is more connected. In fact, the more sounds you make the longer you will be able to ride the orgasmic wave as the sound further stimulates your orgasms and intimate areas. You can use your hands to lightly trace the movements, until you are able to use your awareness. The voice has been shut down for many, fear of being heard, shame for being too primal in the bedroom, and it is time for the throat and pelvis to open. This is vital for both men and women as many men have been shut down and are ready to roar. Perhaps, record this and listen as you guide you.

For the Women

Lay on your back and breathe deep into your belly. As you breathe in fill up the lower belly and as you breathe out, exhale through an open mouth. You will be massaging the breast tissue even if you've had a mastectomy still touch this area with deep love, respect and honour. If the nipples are there, circle them and alternating the style of touch (light, soft and firm). Stay with massaging the nipples and the breasts or place your hands over your chest. Bring your awareness into your breath. Firstly, exhale and relax your whole body, take a deep inhale and follow the inhale breath all the way towards your yoni. Exhale out of your yoni, then inhale from the feet, up the thighs, across the vulva, clitoris and up over the belly and keep drawing the energy up arriving at the breasts. As the breath reaches the breasts exhale out of the nipples, with a sound which comes from deep in your belly with an *ooooohhh sound*. This ooooh sound can be interchanged with the sound *Haaaaaaaa*. Allow the moan to come up and from deep in your belly. Be patient and relax whilst enjoying beginning to open. Keep tracing the breath

Keep tracing with your awareness the breath up and down your body whilst sending loving thoughts to the breast tissue and scar tissue left from a mastectomy. This is healing, and emotions may arise so allow them to be seen, heard and expressed. Remember to allow your throat to open with a moan of 'Ooohhh' on the exhale. This is not about touching the genitals, the breath is sensual, and this is vital to shift beyond sexual and into sensual.

Your sacred yoni begins to open from your heart, free of thought.

For the Men

Lie down on your back and breathe deep into your belly. As you breathe in, fill up the lower belly, and as you breathe out, exhale through an open mouth, relax the belly. Gentle you're your hand of choice as if you are cupping your genitals. Follow your breath with your awareness and begin breathing into the perineum (the soft-sensitive place between the testicles and anus), draw the energy up the testicles and over Your entire lingam, across your belly and towards your chest, feel the energy spreading across the chest and as you exhale, the breath leaves the body through the mouth focusing upon the heart.

Repeat, and cycle again starting at the perineum, drawing up and then exhaling with an open mouth, moan with a HAAAA! Get vocal and moan. This is a powerful exercise of breath to bring the lifeforce energy and pure intention into the heart for deep and lasting intimate connection, with self.

It is the divine lingam that is a doorway to open a man's heart and it is his responsibility to learn to move the energy beyond his genitals through delayed gratification and a spiritual practice of learning how to shift beyond lustful desires and to retain his semen.

These can be practised with your beloved where light touch in introduced, in rhythm with the breath of the one being touched and honoured. Movement, breath, sound and touch combined assist healing the body suit with the life force energy.

Divine union and a perfect fit into one another

Intimacy Rituals in Coupling

Cosmic breath with your Beloved

As with the Yoni-verse exercise sit opposite one another, legs open and straddled with space in-between. Connect with your breath, then with one another's eyes and allow your breaths to synchronise and harmonise.

Feel the energy of the sensual essences connecting and with no touching draw his energetic lingam into you. As you exhale feel your yoni breathing into him. After all, in the yoni-verse ritual you may feel the cosmic lingam and the cosmic yoni, as the cosmic sensual pulse. This is super powerful and may be the deepest connection many will have ever experienced. This can be explored with same sexes as it is a connection with the Spirit bodies. Never be afraid to explore.

You can explore and play here, imagining that you have the other genitals. There is much to explore and to remember that each breath is a sensual caress of the cosmos. This is a great visual and then to bring into coupling with penetration and not a domination of thrusting by the masculine, that is the ego!

Playful and Healthy Sensation Exploration

- Lightly run a feather across your skin, allow the waves of pleasure to flow through your entire being.

- Take some water, lightly pouring bits all over the body. Feel into the sensations- do this with a friend or partner.

- Take warm oil and drip it down your chest, back and tops of thighs and begin to slowly rub it into your skin. Feel into the slippery silkiness of its warmth upon your body and notice how the slipperiness feels like sex. Pause and feel into that. Own it all and explore your many levels of explorative pleasure.

- Grab ice cubes, placing the cold into your warm mouth, suck on the rock cold hardness of the ice. Take it in your fingers and run it all over your body. How does it feel? Is there somewhere warm and special you love to be touched. Run it over every inch of your genitals. Explore, play and be curious! Become the ice and one with it.

Chapter 7: A Flowering Yoni

> *"You are magnificent beyond measure, perfect in your imperfections and wonderfully made"* - Abiola Abrams

The Womb- a sacred place

The womb is both life and death affirming. We enter into this Earth realm by a womb, and we are breathed back into the spirit world through our energetic womb. The womb is the great pulse of life, emanating from within the depths of the womb of God (Sophia). The beautiful womb teaches the art of letting go, to surrender all control and dive deeper into in to the wild and uncontrollable throws of life. The menstrual cycle of a woman is such an event and each month we get to recreate a fresh way forward. A time to let go, dissolve resistance and allow the powerful force of the body held in in pain, and to explore the wisdom revealing within each wave of the uterine walls, a magical time for ancient codes to wash over us and transmute into rich creativity. The attempt to hold on, to numb and control will intensify the waves. It is a time for surrender and the most magical time of a woman's cycle. Begin to see your bleed with a new language of love for your body as pain is a sacred messenger, a beautiful wave of infinite possibilities.

There is a strong link between the menstrual moon tides in women and the tides of the lunar moon, with many women are in synch with the moon. Women living within the same home as friends will often have their lunar cycles in synch. There is deep womb wisdom that has been downloading and is getting ready to be shared with women that are ready to go even deeper, into their power. A woman has 13 menses a year. The womb ovulates on the 13th day, so life is created in the 13th portal. For thousands of years in many cultures, priestesses of the sacred rose have sat in circles of 12, with the 13th being the guide. The womb is the sacred rose, and every woman holds the sacred rose within her. 2018-2021 has seen a rising of the feminine and remembering her rose lineage. This is a key to guiding the sacred masculine into the evolving Earth, a harmonising and re-balancing as Mother Gaia's womb, the cosmic womb and the womb within all, align at this time of feminine consciousness.

An arch that represents the passage of the sacred vagina

Today, 21st June 2021 is the Solstice and there is a shift in frequency, a rebirth of the planet, the cosmos as fresh beginnings arise from the death of the ego. The awakened human upon this refined planet emerges, as we rise as pure loving Souls.

Both men and women have an energetic menstruation, think of it as a *letdown* where they can discover the magnetic, magnificent and infinite power of creation we hold within us, which is in a flux of constant renewal and restoration. What a beautiful opportunity to release and let go, to connect deeply with the feminine moon pole, to exhale and trust and for a man to dive into the depths of his emotional body (the feminine) This is when your soul is free to express the creative and imaginative forces weave into a magnificent blossom. Men may be aligned and in synchronisation with their beloved, honour this time of going deeper into Self, as it is different for all, there is no right or wrong way.

Holding on to what was or an inability to let go of the past will lead to imbalances, pain and this disharmony is flavoured with control and smelling in fear. Overtime this is a toxic environment for the body, leading to illness and dis-ease and this is the state many on the planet are bound in.

The mystical awakening of the womb brings the masculine and feminine energies back into sacred balance and divine union. A vital piece to the puzzle as is this evolutionary shift in consciousness. The womb is the primal creative centre, the seeds of our ideas, visions and dreams, the powerful feminine of manifestation. It is a time for deep introspection, and I am of the belief of resting on your Moon flow (no work) and being in creation is an aspect to healing humanity and honouring the rhythms of the cycles, as the Feminine Keepers of this Sacred Earth. It is a time for women to gather, share wisdom, nourish one another and a time for supporting rites of passage for girls becoming women. The menstrual cycle for many has been viewed as dirty, which is the opposite of this sacred elixir of pure lifeforce. Menstruation is a magical celebration and an honoring of the feminine wisdom. The healing of the womb within men and women is vital in restoring love and respect for Mother Gaia, a representation of the feminine. The V-shape denotes the sacred vagina. The downward pointing triangle symbolises the yoni doorway and there are many sacred sites upon Gaia that hold powerful energy lines. These are often represented by mounds and entrances into the sacred womb -tombs as in caves. These places revered by ancient cultures as magical spaces of life and spiritual rebirth and the entrances often covered by brambles or kept secret. Pubic hair acts to protects the yoni passageway of the Mother Goddess and when she is ready to open, she will without any force. Her golden sweet nectars will flow with ease as her magnificent doorways open to guide deep into her warm darkness.

Reclaiming Your Womb

Many women are unaware of the energetic chords and bonds that remain in a woman's womb space post sexual intercourse with another Soul. Even the lustful desires directed at a woman are felt on a deep core level, and it is time beloved sisters that you call back what is still left outside of your body and sacred womb space. Your womb is sacred, and this is also for every man reading this. You have a spiritual womb that has been fed off, women lusting your seed and to re-claim back your sacred energy. The *Spiritual womb* is known as the *Hara* point, a central point of lifeforce energy, and it is situated in the soft part of the belly and just above the pubic bone. The womb is the source of all creation. It is rich and fertile with a birthing of creative ideas, and this is the spirit of your wild imagination. We all came from the womb, and we shall all return to the womb, submerged into darkness.

Clearing Old Contracts

Find a quiet place to be left undisturbed, close your eyes, connect with your breath and relax. Begin to slowly drop down and into your heart space. As best as you can let go of all thoughts, empty your mind and feel into the essence of pure love.

Imagine there is a circle all around you, and one by one you are going to visualise a soul you have had sex with. See him or her in front of you with love and compassion and call back in the energy that is still there. Think of the energy as being like candy floss, and you are pulling it back from them and bring it back into you and the grounding it into your womb space. If there is some dark energy that feels off, then you can leave it with them and move onto the next. Sending love, compassion and swiftly move on. Keep moving onto the next until you feel you have re-claimed back that energy. Energy is felt and this is why this must always be with a high vibration of love, as it will be felt.

If you feel an angry charge or sadness with a soul doing this, then investigate what it is coming from and attend to your own inner wounds. Then when you are ready re-visit this exercise. Yes, it can bring up feeling of letting go and severing the chord of energy. I am simply, showing you a way how to re-claim your divinity as a soul. Have no attachment to what was, be very business-like with this. Get your boss-truth- badass-bitch on and have fun with this. The key is to not get drawn into the emotions and another drama which you can potentially create!

"Your lives are interwoven into the beautiful tapestry of live, to reconnect, open, remember, express your gifts and embrace all aspects of Self. Mirrors all interwoven into the intricate web of life". - Zoe-Anna

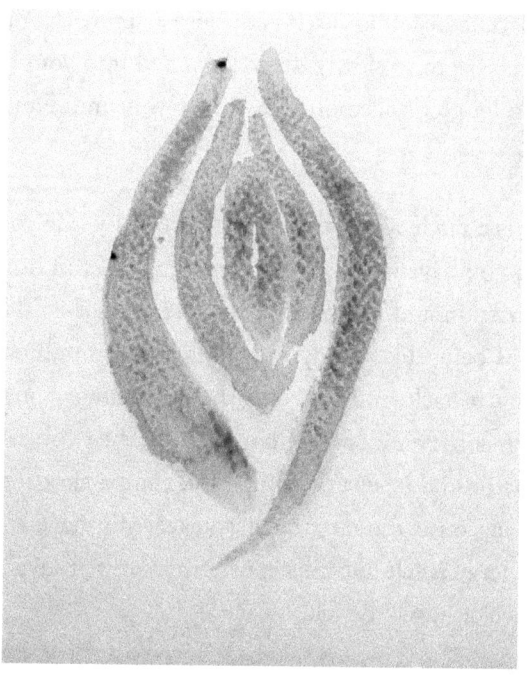

Sacred life force elixir of my womb flow in art creations

THE BLOOD MYSTERIES

I have been honoured to share sacred sensual explorations of an intertwining between the physical and spiritual realms, tasting into an expanded state of pure bliss. Each occasion was a divine union full of deep soul love naturally guided by Spirit. Each experience opened the doorway to 'bliss', call it intuitive wisdom guiding with curious innocence. As a Maverick, I explore experiences, gain insights and then the knowledge is presented by a brother or a sister. This confirms knowledge gained via direct discovery. The next phase is a deeper reflection into the knowledge which births inner wisdom of knowing and DNA remembrance.

If you are a woman that still bleeds her monthly moon flow, then have a release. There is magic in the crone phase as when the moon flow ceases the sage wisdom remains and sensual essence expands and continues to move upwards as no longer leaving the body in a moon flow. There is a transition that many of you may be going through as you bleed, and the crone wisdom is revealing to you. Womanhood is a gift we are blessed with to dive deeper into the hypnotic waves of ancient wisdom calling you deeper into your Womb. Honour this sacred place, as the holy temple that it is.

The womb is the portal of life and death and each mandala you see in nature is a representation of the womb and a portal into realms beyond the naked eyes. The cervix is an eye of clear seeing into the Stars and cosmos.

This is a time where women would gather in tribe and sacred circles to nourish, bathe and celebrate one another. How times changed and how we are coming home. Home translating to *Here on Mother Earth*.

During this hypnotic state of the first few days of my moon flow, creativity was being called to express. Honour your own inner wise guidance of your sacred womb moment to moment. Times of deep surrendering brought me to my knees upon the Earths flesh. I cried, groaned and moaned deep into the primal wounds and wisdom of being blessed as a Woman. It is my intention to guide You how to pivot with fluidity and grace moment to moment and honour each message. To retreat into your darkness and inner landscape no matter the external environment. You and I together we rise.

The messages that present take focus, courage and patience to begin to live life is a very different way. To courageously leap into the dark unknown of limitless wisdom and the sacredness of being a woman.

Here are some healthy and beneficial ways to explore with your own sacred moon flow. Here are some practices that I dedicate sacred time and space to honour, as this is your own lifeforce. It is your ceremony, and you came here to explore shamelessly.

Moon Practices

- Collecting from my moon cup – from day 1 to the end of my flow
- Womb Art – Allow inner wisdom to guide and draw, using my blood to paint with
- Using my menstrual flow on my face at night – Replenishes stem cells of the face
- As a face mask at night – it tightens and plumps the skin by the morning
- Wearing specific jewelry only when I am having my monthly bleed
- Having more time alone for journaling my dreams at night

- Giving some of my monthly bleed back to Mother Gaia, at the base of a tree
- Placing a drop of my menstrual flow under my tongue
- Placing blood upon specific areas of my body in self-ceremony
- Minimise work on these days and be open for creative flow.
- I am introspective and silent, often having creative downloads.

Menstrual blood is not demonic, it is sacred and sadly, what is pure has been misused, misguided and this is something I am passing on within sacred womb circles. Periods are not dirty and to pour this sacred elixir down the toilet is not honouring its sacred gift it brings to women that are still having their monthly moon flow. Painful periods can be caused by fear of letting go and congestion in the pelvic and yoni tissues of a woman. The pain is a messenger, the blocked area a doorway, all to reveal deeper messages and womb wisdom.

Like anything that it pure, is can also be used for darkness and evil. Welcome to polarity, where there will always be potential for distortions. This is pure light beyond anything demonic.

The feast of the Gods, tasting into and the sweetest sensual dew and interestingly, a practice that was condemned by the church and seen as sinful, shameful and dirty! Interestingly, in 2020 much began to be revealed of occult dark practices, lifeforce energy being misused, manipulated to access power and superpowers, as in Satanic Ritual Acts. I am calling this out, as what I am about to share is wisdom that is of the light, and has been hidden, made shameful by the church, and yet this it is an embodiment of light and pure love. As a Star seed of Pleiades, it was the Pleiadian teachings that resonated with my heart and soul, like a deep inner knowing. It was from my personal and innocent experiences that I gained many direct insights later confirmed by Barbara Marciniak.

According to EARTH- Pleiadian Keys to the Living Library- by Barbara Marciniak (1995), we are in a time of remembering and a woman's substance of power is in her menstrual blood flow, while the substance of power for a man is his sperm (Fertile sperm –non-vasectomy). Blood is said to be the elixir for healing and a source of life, revitalisation and regeneration. When you share these in a loving and bonded relationship it is the ultimate feast of sharing your secret powers. The highest honour for a King and his Queen, a blending of identities to remember whom you are and why in this lifetime you have come back together. It is the most magical and beautiful experience, menstrual blood mixed with semen and vaginal juices then painting one another in ceremony and licking in from one another, to drink from her cup with their nectars mixed together, blood and sensual juices, it is the sweetest taste to be enjoyed. As you ingest and share in this powerful and potent mix, you are within a state of love; trust and the deepest gates of bonding are flung open into orgasmic bliss states. Deal with menstrual blood as you would be the awareness of any bodily fluid, this is a sacred act and not to take lightly. This can be alchemised between beloveds to have mixed into a sublingual elixir to maintain their sacred love connection unified in light and taken by both daily.

Menstrual blood has a metallic taste when smelt in a cup and may smell strong the first time you place it onto your skin and face. A woman's menstrual blood flow is loaded with the substance D.M.T, which is an indication of the expanded consciousness that is within her menses every month, and for many this is poured unknowingly into the sewerage system. A woman's body is designed to experience these levels of awareness every month, enabling her to reach the expanded levels of consciousness and the unified field. D.M.T has been called the 'spirit molecule', used in Shamanic rituals as a brew made from specific plants, used for healing purposes and the hallucinogenic effects. A woman produces these substances naturally. This is released from the woman's pituitary gland, which brings the sacredness and powerful time for a woman. This is a sacred time of being closest to the Divine Mother. This cycle is the re-birth and death, a cleansing of old ideas, old patterns of negativity and surrender allowing the divine to flow through. This is a woman's time of deep inner purification, ready to receive the new fresh ideas. This honouring and becoming aware of the sacredness to her moon flow she begins to re-ignite the deep bonds of the divine mother. This is a journey to wholeness and a state of deep inner healing and health. There are blood mysteries that I am continuing to explore as the Sharman within leads the way into the darkness and the mystical unknown. I like many of you, have walked this path many times before. There is wisdom that is to remain sacred and passed on, woman to woman and I feel woman to man. After all we are in the transition of leaving an era of male domination. These mysteries are held safe as mysteries of wisdom for a reason, and they are not to be manipulated by the feminine to lure and control men as this is nefarious in nature. We have done the witch burning, lets rise above it and accept that the most potent of wisdom naturally un-locks with a soul and the sacred feminine is to be protected.

Bliss is our highest state of being.

I am poetic and unapologetic in design.

Chapter 8: Awakening & Conscious Relationships

> *"Sexuality and sensuality are completely different things. Sensuality is something that you're born with. But sexuality is something that I leave for my own mirror."* - Ricky Martin

Expanding Sensuality

Welcome to the expanding relationship and my personal perspective into the sensual revolution and evolutions in consciousness in regard to relationship. There are right and wrong actions in life, and I am not here to sway your choices or be the judge. I am simply opening up different flavours to get curious by allowing your heart to lead and give yourself permission to explore beyond what you know (in the mind and whatever happens next). My point is, read this with an open mind beyond opinion and see a bigger picture that is playing out. Sensuality is your right to explore and what that means to You. No matter where you are currently at, life presents the most aligned teachers and experiences to mirror and reflect what your deepest fears and shadows are.

We are all learning, and we will all graduate. Attitudes around sex and sensuality are changing moment to moment. It is my intention to encourage wise discernment as you go embark upon your sensual adventure and the journey of inner healing to knowing thy self. Have your eyes and ears wide open to the internal messages of instinct beyond the performance of the visual. Remember, this is a sensual adventure of innocence.

> *My sexuality has never been a problem to me, but I think it has been for other people*
>
> - Dusty Springfield

There has been a sensual awakening and revolution of freedom happening, which reminds me of the 'free-loving 60's'. I am not saying I am all for the swinging 60's as I feel this was a dilution of life force and I will outline in this chapters that which I have direct insight into. There was a shift in 2015, and intimacy gained more exposure and exploration into 2021. Souls began to explore what it means to live a life of freedom with trust and honesty in their relationships. I believe many relationships are going through a massive redesign as Souls are feeling dissatisfied in love, be it a dysfunctional relationship with self or with their intimate other. Souls are beginning to follow what it is they desire which may no longer be in a long-term committed relationship as there is greater freedom of choice and openness being explored.

I see men and women seeking intimate connections elsewhere, outside their relationships and this is adding to the burden of a society of guilt and shame. No matter an individual's choice it has to come back to each individual's willingness to be transparent and own all actions. As only then can a soul be free? The porn industry has manipulated the collective, feeding off addictions and sadly adding to the numbness and disconnection from intimacy and real life. This lowers the energetic vibrancy of an individual's lifeforce and the individual is bound in the 3rd density of the trauma patterns and sexual programming in consciousness. No matter if you are gay, straight, coupled or single the effect of your life-life-force impacts the others within the environment that you live in.

The journey begins by working on you every day and courageously following your path. No one or nothing else exterior can re-fuel you. It is not their role!

Be shameless in your free expression of the wild Femme

As part of this sensual (R)evolution there is still shame around sex and held within the tapestry of the collective. This unconsciousness based in fear has to be addressed and brought into the open with love. A pivotal part of the sensual evolution is to know thy self and express you. Own your voice and follow what is aligned, as a sovereign being. I am not you, and you are not me. Choices shift and change, and exploration is your human right. You are a spiritual being having a human experience, and for many of the population you never got to explore in those early adolescent years of innocence. If you are living life below the line in blame, shame and guilt you are yet to grow into adulthood. This picture to me captures the raw messiness within intimacy between two people and having a safe place to express all ranges of your sexual expression beyond shame, guilt and for a woman to explore all aspects of her wild free expression. You may each have a different opinion and I have not added it here to titillate the men, see the art and innocence within the picture.

GROWING INTO ADULTHOOD

- Ownership
- Accountability
- Responsibility
- Restraint

As you shift the way of showing up for your life, everyone around you will be impacted. Open disclosure is vital to be in truth, honesty and integrity. No more hiding what you desire and want to explore in life. Taking self-responsibility is the ultimate door towards inner freedom.

> *"If repression has indeed become the fundamental link between power, knowledge and sexuality since the classical age; it stands to reason that we will not be able to free ourselves from it except at a considerable cost."* - Michel Foucault

BEHIND THE SCENES

Let's be honest; the emotional devastation and carnage of a divorce impacts children no matter how smooth or messy the process. Divorce rates have increased and many households now co-parent. The younger generation has witnessed this, and many are finding the idea of marriage less desirable. Added to these options of opportunities have flung wide open and a desensitisation of human connection. Courting and getting to know someone through human connection is playing at both ends of the scale, some teenagers/young adults are seeing the importance of getting to know the other and not rushing the process and then those replacing organic connection by online dating apps of convenience. Swipe left, swipe right, yes, the online meat markets of dating, it has become all about looks, how convincing your profile is and frankly much is fake and superficial. Dating apps for many have become the easy options for getting laid and feeding underlying loneliness. It is feeding societies disconnection; dissociation and it feeds off the human psyche and spirit much like porn!

Real connection with transparent presence is dying. Even family dinners happen less and less. People are being too busy to connect, with time poor choices and working longer hours. Once one clicks on a profile then it is the physical superficial traits that have to grab your attention in the first 2-seconds. This leads to fake personas and a picture that look nothing like the person. This is the de-evolution in sensuality and disconnection all warming you up to AI and a doorway for entities to feed off your sacred life force.

This next part is an extract from a presentation by Mark Passio on the *'Unholy Feminine' – Neo-feminism & the Satanic Epi-Eugenics Agenda*. A brilliant presentation which you can find on YouTube, and this is a very small aspect of his phenomenal expertise and delivery.

'Japan is being called the *'epidemic intimacy crisis'* and has the fastest declining population rates in the world. Almost half the population of Japan claims that it is no longer interested in any kind of sexual intimacy. This is happening because of destroyed sex drive in both genders due to extremely low testosterone levels. Japan is merely the social engineer's testing ground for their depopulation agenda.

The American Intimacy Crisis has already begun. It is just unspoken and is not likely to make headline news in mainstream media.'

50% people 16-49 no sex in past month

27% men not interested in any sex

23% of women not interested in any sex

61% men 18-34 not in relationship

49% women 18-34 not in relationship

36% men 18-34 have never had sex

39% women 18-34 never has sex

This is alarm bells concerning on a global scale and just scrapes the surface of one of the biggest agendas for de-humanisation and the rise of asexualisation. Asexual people are those that do not experience sexual attraction to anyone else. Asexualisation is characterised by a total disinterest in all sexual behaviour. This is another example of what social engineering and low testosterone levels in men and women will create. Testosterone is a vital hormone for natural sexual drive for both sexes and you don't have to see how obesity is also an added factor to low levels of desire.

Society has become numb, dissatisfied, complacent, superficial and lonely. These apps and the AI on the apps are replacing healthy human interaction. This is also something that was rolling out in Japan, where teenagers and young adults had a bot/AI girlfriend or AI boyfriend and would be seen out on dates with their phone date, and it was a social norm amongst youth and young adults.

If this doesn't wake you up then you are numb and perhaps, already dead! – Zoe

Many adults are removing primal connection via natural attraction by removing all body hair. Your body hair secretes pheromones and acts as an antenna radiating electromagnetic information connecting and communicating with the environment. Many are so overloaded in aftershave and perfumes that you can no longer smell the true essence of sweat mixed with emotions on the skin. Shaving, waxing or lasering pubic hair impacts warrior strength, courage and natural responses for primal attraction. Sensitive tissues are de-sensitised by lasers, adding to the underlying numbness of this sensitive tissue. Society is becoming less human as they have become socially conditioned in obedience and avoidance of taking responsibility to grow through meeting the pain, discomfort and loneliness. They are programed with fear, reacting out of the reptilian brain of Survival and have yet to learn how to take responsibility for their emotions. You can only evolve to the level of the brain and then sexual energy is life giving and a key to raising consciousness and human evolution. You have to be willing to face your fears, do the inner work and meet the unconsciousness of your ignorance. The rebels, the artists, poets and freedom speakers have higher testosterone as they step up for what is right. Low testosterone impacts desire and will reduce survival. It is vital to learn how to adapt and evolve no matter how the external world shifts and stop placing blame on your circumstances. Be willing to step out of line and think for yourself and be the weaver of your own dreams.

Porn and paying for sex were at a record high prior to the so-called pandemic of 2020. Special offers were given for online porn sites, and it was fascinating how bottle shops were doing the same. Both are ways to feed the numbness, feed the addiction of loneliness and keep those trapped in codependency. Though it never gets talked about the porn industry serves a 1/3 of the global population. That is a massive wake-up. This is a ploy all to keep the sleepwalkers numb, dumb and blowing cum with a low vibration of addiction and over-sexualisation of the feminine and masculine bound by lust and desire. The dehumanization and depopulation agenda in full swing, and most are blind (ig-norance) to it all. This is a sad contrast to sacred sensuality and a heart connection between two humans in a love-based union.

What is Spiritual Connection?

One of the most powerful spiritual connections is found within infinite Source love. This may be by aligning with the cosmic energy of the cosmos or devotion to God and does not have to include another human being. Consciousness is love and not the fluffy kind of love or that as in relationship. Love is the creative force of all life and the raising of consciousness beyond the genitals, and this is the path of sacred sensuality. This connection begins with Self and others will feel it, attempt to feed off it and any access through empty sex is potential for depletion and draining of sacred life force energy. Forgive yourself for poor judgement and learn from the experiences. This is how we learn, grow and evolve as a species.

A spiritual connection involves aligning all levels of mind, body and spirit whilst tuning into all physical senses of your emotional and spiritual wellbeing. Within this mutually synchronistic realm words cannot begin to describe the rich feelings of epic potency! There is a weaving of life-force energies, and this level of spiritual connection takes concentration and skillful practice, without getting lost in the sexual heightened explosion of the orgasm.

With the highest of intention of wholeness as love, the trilogy of body-mind and spirit infuses for that moment in time. This connection is where each soul's cup over-flows in infinite love, passion and joy, and not from half empty. Only share what you feel comfortable sharing and what overflows, allow others to drink from your saucer as the contents of your cup are sacred, holy and it may burn those that are not ready for its elixir. To share one another's cups that overflow into one vessel is unity and meeting in the ocean of love, trust and oneness.

The interplay of each individual expressing this life-force is dependent upon physical movement, connection with nature, mindset, emotionality, sound, hydration and the foods you eat. To assess instinctual ability to use your entire senses, taste, smell, touch, sight, and sound within the experience.

This is what Tantra means to me. Devotion to Great Spirit, Source, God and devoted to serving as a conduit for love radiance to express through. I am devoted to serve as I am guided moment to moment and to with a Soul that is devoted to truth. Love is the only Truth.

To be living and expressing as a spiritual being is a sensual experience. Master this first, the union of the masculine and feminine forces within self. As the ability to cultivate this level of connection firstly begins in the mind. To embody this, you have to un-fu#k your mind to be Sovereign and free.

To experience spiritual connection a practice of focus and concentration is key. This develops and strengthens will power, and that is why the practice of meditation is key in the tantric awakening. Having never studied a formal training of Tantra, it was the years of Vedic meditation practices, the movement of the body and breathwork that unleashed the Tantric wisdom, and all that tantra embodies.

I became connected with all wisdom and an empty vessel for the divinity of light and Source to flow through. A conduit for pure love.

WHAT IS BLOCKING SPIRITUAL CONNECTION?

Your mind, the past, addictions to porn, sexual programming and unresolved trauma in the body are all blocking the connection to spirit. You are born sovereign, so you have the ability to reach this deep connection as it begins with the willingness to embark upon your spiritual journey. To rewire the fears, patterns and strive towards mastery of self-love!

The mind blocks and limits your capacity to transcend deeper into the embodied sensual experience with another soul. The fears, limiting beliefs and lack of trust (in Self) translates to not being able to trust another. The mind awaits in external judgment usually with many speculations. Many are unaware of the other possibilities as they are only focused on the experience with a narrowed view of perception which blocks clear viewing of the truth. Reality is truth and you cannot see truth from a narrowed view of your perception. Life creates more of the unwanted events until you see that it is time to change the way you see things and the meaning you give them. You cannot feel until you are willing to explore the pain and then feel into the pain to experience the emotions and from the emotions be ready to evolve in the spiritual path of knowing thy self.

Get honest and get clear on what you want and desire in life by peeling back the layers of the shitshow and exploring the inner shadows work of Self. It is your mission to know you and seek knowledge and with the awareness, implement to unveil the unconsciousness programs with diligent loving awareness. It is vital to shift any external perception you think is reality by having the courage to explore the darkness of the inner world of You. These shadows are ugly, and you may want to reject them, and it is time to sit with them all. In order to grow, you have to reveal each shadow to heal and transform each into a gift. These are keys to your inner and outer reactions and the patterns of behaviour playing out in your past and present-day life. Looking for sacred sensuality outside of self without implementing some form of shadow work may feel like you are stuck in the same cycle of self-destruct, as what your heart seeks remains an illusion.

> *Existing in infidelity, lies, shame, blame, guilt, jealousy and sin will suffocate your Soul*
>
> Zoe Bell

A Conscious Divine Union

Many are choosing a time of abstinence, from self-pleasure and sex, this is a path of remembrance of Sovereignty. If you are jumping from relationship to another, this will be a great practice to pause and heal what is out of balance. Begin to notice where you freely give your sensual energy away or feed off by others sensual energy. You have to own where you have mis-used the sovereignty of your sacred womb space by ignoring your instinct and where you have not respected another's space. No matter the event, it all comes back to you.

It is a vital time in your conscious evolution to restore the imbalances in Self first. This period of abstinence allows transmutation of the old physical 3rd dimensional programming of lust and sexual addictions/ habits that do not honour the sacredness of the feminine vessel. This deep dive through the spiral and to prepare for awakening into the sacred heart. To dive deeper into the magical mystery tours of self, requires solitude of alone time with no external distractions and no masturbation. A process of learning how to trust in life and learning how to work with the sacred healing energy of consciousness. These external distractions are ways to fill up on the numbness and pain. This is the shift of 2021 that consciousness is going through, the leap and transition into the sacred heart.

For her, this is about disconnecting from the programs of performance, for example, the *'damsel in distress'*, and the *'Slut-sex-slave program'* to men. A time to reconnect to the sacredness of her energy and allow her body-mind to become re-connected to Self as source. For him, it is a time to detach from his stance of performance, for example the *'Saviour and knight in shining armour program'* and the *'sex god/stud'* program. This will allow him to reconnect to his body-mind-to align with Self as Source. This releasing of the matrix programs of control, power and domination to begin to re-align with the true essence of learning about Sacred Sensuality.

Choose abstinence and if it feels aligned withhold self-pleasure and start to work with the sexual energy and move it up the body rather than staying stuck in the genitals. Allow pubic and armpit hair to grow and see how that feels in your freedom. Stop apologising for not removing your hair for another, all to feel accepted, sexy and enough. The shackles of social conditioning run deep for women, and they begin to drop away as the shadow aspects of self are revealed. The clever games of manipulation, seduction and performance all to get fleeting desires met. A total purification and re-setting and attending to the inner energies.

A Queen and badass warrior Bitch. Bitch, meaning, 'babe-in-total-control-(of)-herself.'

Each soul explores a journey back to source and the divine union within. True love making is the merging of two souls, where two become one. The act of copulation is in fact, secondary. The true connection is the Sacred Union itself.

Her power is felt in her womb, and his power found in his heart. This is the reason why the human man was driven to get into her yoni, and she was driven to find a way into his heart. This shifts from duality into union within. This is for both the physical man and the physical woman. This sacred union begins with our own union of the sacred masculine and the sacred feminine, and the experience felt is the cosmic orgasm. This inward journey is being willing to explore the solitude and dissolve old programs of conditioning of performance and false expectations. This journey of sacred sexuality is freedom and is what will heal the rage held in humanity in regard to sensuality.

You are the way showers, the freedom fighters that have developed your angel wings, one called of trust and the other, faith, in self. I am here to co-create as a divine expression of pure love, as together we rise as One. May this be a quantum leap for many as humanity is calling out.

Co-Creating a Symbiotic Relationship

Many are shifting and awakening in consciousness and may be exploring a symbiotic relationship, or perhaps wanting this. This is a sacred connection that infuses deep spiritual love, heart to heart within the stable foundations of presence with transparency. A magical blend of spiritual essences interwoven together, heightening sensitivities towards a telepathic and empathetic connection.

Both are looking for a partner who is on the journey to evolve, at times together and in their own unique way, honouring their own space. There is a magnetic spiritual connection infused with sensual alchemy. Both are living their passions and expressing their Soul purpose, with no desire or need to overpower or dominate the other as both parties are living with purpose and co-creating great things for humanity and our planet.

This type of connection will only work with two people when there is a natural bonding during lovemaking and orgasm. Spend some time attuning to your personal womb power, inner healing and reclaiming your sovereignty as when the time is right this divine other will be brought to you. This deliberate bonding practice of sexual connection, known as coupling, brings you both closer emotionally, opening the door to intimacy, trust and staying power of magnetism. I don't care what others say, sex-bonding is vital to our species. This is not the pounding motion that you see of the masculine domination over the feminine, that is an old program that is driven by the masculine ego and is not honouring the feminine holy temple. This union has to be built upon a foundation of trust, faith, honesty, love and transparency. As together they can reach higher states of lifegiving cosmic bliss and realms beyond.

This relationship is growing and evolving in all-ways, where there is excitement in both honouring their introspective space as their soul mission leads the way. Both require a high level of emotional intelligence to hold space and the courage to connect deeply and share in a space of raw vulnerability.

I will add this, this relationship may also have more than two people in it. For example, he or she may openly be a *three-coupling conscious relationship*.

Only you will know what is aligned for your soul.

This does not make it less or more conscious, again, it is free will and choice with full disclosure for all parties. When two- or three- people come together with an intention of growth, the relationship strives towards something greater than instant and personal gratification. Romance may flow and intimacy is an aspect of the creative ripple of inspiration. This creates a passionate wave of possibility and is infectiously delicious to be around. This beautiful partnership becomes a journey into soul evolution and is a step towards evolution and inner growth as an individual. You may both start to create new boundaries and rules within your relationship and take responsibility for what you are hiding within. All evolving relationships have to now be built upon honesty and transparency.

To know thy self is a gift and a beautiful love affair to explore.

Co-Existing in Relationship

Are You feeling trapped within a co-existing relationship and running totally different lives? You meet at the end of the day exhausted as your head hits the pillow and you roll away from your partner and go to sleep! Sex is placed on the backburner and excuses have replaced intimacy. Connection with presence has been clouded over with a mist of complacency. A mist of lost hope, holding onto an old story, a past choice that they are unable to express, or an underlying, seething deep bitterness or unspoken loneliness.

Does this sound familiar?

Imagine this. You are two-steam trains travelling through a crazy game of life having a relationship. You both begin at the same place, both afraid of de-railing your own train as you are afraid to rock the track and change lanes. You are both living different lives, and even at the station stop, you both have your busy heads stuck in your digital lives, and all poetic extra-sensory connection has been left in the wake. One train may be over-loaded with emotional baggage and the other stuck in the over-thinking mind, still in the past, at the last stop. One train must 'wake-up' and step up to taking action of their spiritual path. Both are out of sync, making lame empty promise and blaming one another, all to meet external expectations to reach the next station on time. Both of you have lost at this point and forgotten the meaning of living a vibrant life. Perhaps, one may be attending to the other trains wheels, and added to that the carriages (children), and sadly, forgetting about your own direction, and the passion (fire) of your own engine!

This is an experience of the relationship that is going through the motions and the passion has become numb in the heart. Both have forgotten how to connect with self and the spiritual interaction of passion combined with deep connection and excitement they felt at the start. The magnetism of two souls fully engaged and present is replaced by empty love and countless hot air. An angry steam brewing and perfectly aligned to de-rail both in chaos and destruction.

This moment of de-railing is a trigger into experiencing the intoxicating potion of passion, a moment of diffusion, neutrality, zero-point, totally open, connected, present with wild desire for one another. The point between leaving or staying, to realise everything you have and to see all that you have outgrown and all that is slipping away. It feels like living and dying all at the same time, a reminder of the preciousness of life. This opens up a choice and when both are feeling this reciprocal heightened state, make-up sex will naturally follow. This is the most potent elixir as if feels like oxygen for one another's soul. It may feel like a sudden death, as they are about to lose it all. Make-up sex is off the charts and the wildest sex that possibly these souls have every experienced together. This is an example of being free of all attachment, free of any agenda and in total surrender to one another. To bathe and drink into one another's Soul.

Relationships tend to reveal what we cannot see at the time and to reveal what we are ready to understand about Self. Each soul is drawn together for a purpose, a lesson and a reason. Once, you grasp this concept, then it is easier to move on. Gain the insight, and most vital of all address that what is revealed about you! Let's explore relationships where both partners choose to have more of an open status.

OPEN RELATIONSHIPS

When souls meet that are spiritually awake and conscious with free will with no baggage of shame, guilt, then another level of relationship may be experienced. This may lead to lovers and partners to being able to express within a healthy relating relationship.

An 'open relationship' is where both in the relationship are free to have other sexual interactions, and communication, trust and honesty, is a largest aspect of their foundation. They have one another as their stable base and share a deep love for one another.

This may be a transition for couples that have shared many years together, and may be feeling stagnation, and that stepping out and exploring with other souls to add to their spiritual growth and for variety. With any arrangement, communication with trust is the glue that holds them together with a high level of love and mutual respect of agreed boundaries. They may express and share these experiences with one another or may have a profound shift in awareness they wish to communicate, or they may have an agreement of silence. Their love for one another is not less it is how each is choosing to live and show up moment to moment for their lives. This brings us onto the topic of *conscious open relating*. This is an evolutionary leap away from the one-night stand and empty mindless fu*king.

It is time to wake-up and expose a perception of truth that perhaps some in committed monogamous relationships, have secrets in their closet that they do not wish their partner to know about. This is why, open relating is vital to the evolution of the co-created symbiotic relationship. No matter what relationship you choose, open communication, raw vulnerability and honesty are the key. Even in a divine union of sacred sexuality each are free to step away. It is not based on empty fear-based promises, and each are there for as long, or as little as they consciously choose. Free of attachment and the only ownership is upon their own free choices. As any partnership and intimate relationship is never about owning the other, and accountability of choices and responsibility of actions is vital.

A personal experience of conscious relating

Like all personal growth, it is never an easy path, and takes a willingness to get your warrior on, big girl or big boy panties as it may feel like a battlefield of not knowing and uncertainty of the unknown. The only intention is the raw truth of love, by all parties. It is easier and less complicated when there are two souls expressing at this level. This will include removing the masks, the layers of secrets and having the courage to express what is deep in their hearts. It can be scary and yet, at the same time freeing to gain realisation of unprocessed emotions, pent up anger and a closing down of the heart. I will open the door into one of these experiences, to take you on a journey

It was a magical realm to hold presence for one another, and share deep pain, our inner challenges, struggles, and the fear-based projections onto one another. To own the hurt we had caused with one another and see beyond opinion. The pent-up anger was seeking a place to express, and this suffocating of the soul was given a place to be free.

To see the hurt and pain within one another's eyes, and with the desire to quickly wipe the slate and start all over again. Yet, we made a commitment to go deeper. No more tip-tiptoeing around with surface level bullshit, over-apologising with meaningless words.

Listening to his side of the story, was like an explosion of rage deep in my body, as I listened, doing everything I could to contain my side of the conversation. We were on the edge of biting our tongues, and many times found ourselves in headlock, in rage.

After a while of headlock, we found some common ground to witness that what we saw was our own inner reflection. The hurt, the pain, and it was time to let this chapter go, to heal and move on. This next part would be within our own space, alone with our thoughts, on opposite sides of the room. As we were in an open relationship, it was time to look at where we still had sexual energy, and romantic connections, which were driving a force between us. It was time to cut these chords and bring this scattered energy back into our hearts.

To see how we had had an agenda to get one up on one another, it was like we had been pushing one another, testing and retaliating. Each thing we wrote and felt, was all about bringing it back to self. Raw un-cut ownership.

From, the opposite sides of the room we captured one another's gaze, and stood eye to eye, heart to heart, as from the ground we would rise. We took one step towards one another and expressed everything we could take responsibility for what has cause pain and resentment in the relationship. We got to witness one another, owning our shit. The air was thick with potent stillness, and the room was charged with presence. A peaceful ground rather than the battlefield of blood.

The next step, we labelled everything that we were letting go of, the resentments, and the grief within our hearts.

The third step, we expressed what we were was committed to moving forwards, and how we desired to take care of one another. The vulnerability was thick and raw, with not knowing what the other would share. The truth is, this would be a pivotal step in my own evolution as a soul, and a 180-degree flip side-ways. His truth was to walk away, and to not continue walking alongside me. It would be another lesson to heal old remnants of disappointment, and the shadow of attachment.

A pivotal time as my raw heart ripped opened wide into deeper depths.

Open relating is powerful, and this is the (R)evolution for conscious heart-opening in intimate relating. This shifts far beyond sex and is the sacred doorway to explore the depths of the heart.

Perhaps our greatest distinction as a species is our capacity, unique among animals, to make counter-evolutionary choices. - Jared Diamond

DISHONOURING LIFEFORCE

Have you ever had a sexual interaction that left you feeling drained afterwards? This is a strong message to listen to. You may or may not be aware that with each interaction you are receiving spiritual guidance. Do you know which is your intuition and gut response, seeing, hearing and knowing it and then trusting the messages that you are being shown and to reveal the course of action for your highest alignment? It is time to listen and tune in the messages and trust instinct. The feeling of being able to relax and fall asleep next to one another is a sign of trust. If you are unable to sleep next to them, with one eye open all night then this is a sign of you higher self is communicating that it is not safe falling asleep. Either that or he or she needs a new bed that you enjoy sleeping in!

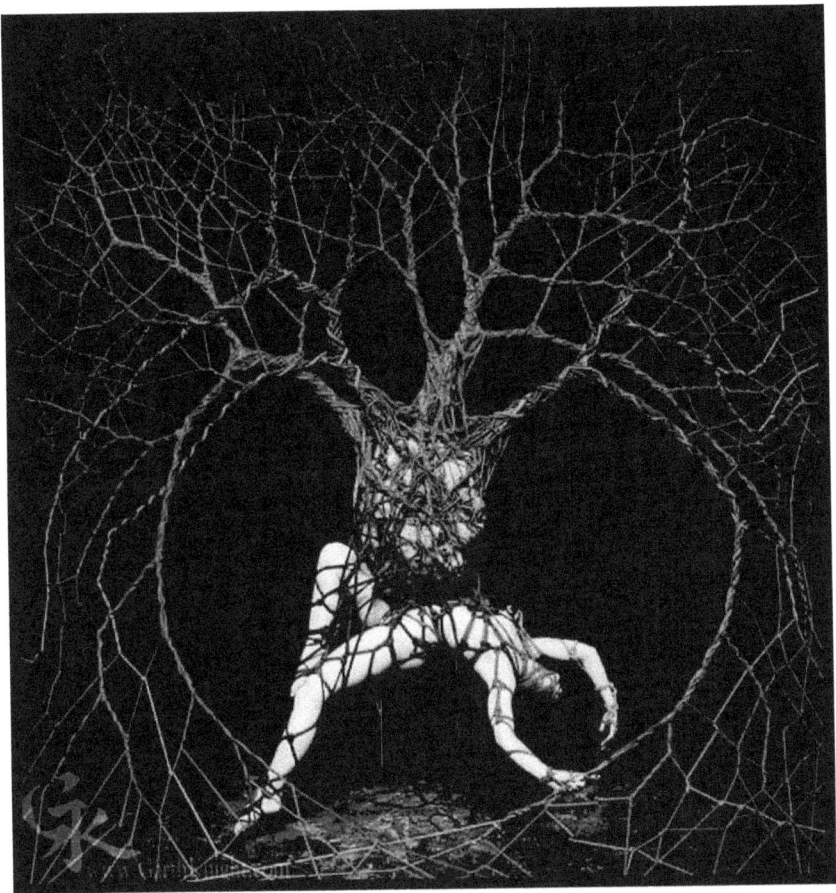

Life is a series of lessons to grow into adulthood

- Have no regrets with your choices
- Never blame the other for your choices
- Be shameless and wiser next time
- Courageously gain insight and learn from experiences
- Practice open relating by expressing your heart

- Self-love and responsibility for clearing your energy
- Honour your boundaries & be comfortable alone in your own space
- Be true to you in every way as it is easier to be true to others!

NON- MONOGAMY

This where souls are choosing not to be in a relationship or are in an open relationship with other sexual unions, rather than one intimate partner.

This is alignment of two souls that are totally present with one another, intertwining caught up within a bubble of lust. It is lust and not love.

Some believe and feel this is where we are evolving too. Some have the belief and ponder the question, are we meant to be monogamous as a species? Whatever you believe will be your perception within the experience.

This level of soul connection can only be achieved in the now with no reference to the past or future.

With any sexually and intimate interaction there will be a deep transference of exchange of energy, which will be more profound for the one being penetrated, vaginally or anally. When another man dips his lingam (penis) into the potent nectar of the sweet yoni (vagina), where there is no condom, DNA is left from bodily fluids. Cleansing and clearing your body are vital and knowing which energy to cut and which to keep. Energy can still remain even with a condom. DNA can remain there for seven-years and may need to be cleared during womb healing, sensual yoni massage session, and shamanic energy healing.

A spiritually evolved man and woman will feel, taste and smell the energies that have been there before.

During any exchange of orgasms, you are exchanging energy frequencies and open yourself up to exchanging entities. I've experienced this a few times, so be mindful of sexually transmitted demons along with sexually transmitted disease. This will be explored in greater depth within 'Soul Codes' and how sexual intercourse is meant to enhance your soul codes as part of your soul evolutionary journey. In all acts of intimacy with orgasm you will have other beings enjoying the human experience of sex, as they are learning and upgrading DNA and codes. This may freak some out, it is not my intention as you always can ask an energy to leave. Remember you are not the only ones learning in the universe.

There is a difference once you raise your level of consciousness and intimate coupling requires wise discernment to smell the other to ensure you are both vibrating with pure intention. Be wise and take responsibility in all choices and forgive yourself when you fuck up and own it all.

The only relationship to master is the spiritual relationship with the You-niverse, know thy self and know the universe. Keep coming back to you, no matter what happens and share your free-Queen-see with the world. Be ever-present within the changing tides of life and remember no one belongs to anyone. Everything is choice and everyone has the ability to strengthen free will and each choice of free will has a consequence. Live with integrity and follow the principles of nature and spirit to choose the right path that brings no harm to others and when threatened and your voice not honoured, know when to draw your sword of truth to protect your sacred sovereignty and freedom or self and all those that you love.

WILDFLOWER

Free will of passion

Her heart rips open free & wide

A pure ecstasy bbubbles up inside.

A tribal dance awakened within

Her soul expressing

Free will of spirit,

Never to hide, again.

She draws him in close

With her mystical gaze

As he melts her soul

Warm Souls embrace.

Their bodies entwined

Gyrating to the beat

Tribal stomping of their feet

Boundless and sensual

Suspended in time

AWAKENING & CONSCIOUS RELATIONSHIPS

They move as one
Upon the dance floor
With no other needs
Except sweet bliss of joy.

Tenderness abounds
The full moon holding space
Shines upon
Her glowing sensual grace.

For many souls - a sweet embrace
For within their passion
A fire burns bright
Reflected within, and as without

Her inner glow forever bright
An intoxicating allure,
Throughout the night
The full moon ablaze.

WILDFLOWER

Beating upon

Their beautiful bodies

Embracing tones

As they become one.

Nothing to stop

Their burning passion

An ignited glow

New Earths fashion.

United in love holding hands

With compassion.

Within their flow,

The sweet nectar of life

Bubbling forth into the night.

His lips are soft

As he drinks in her kisses

Their cups are full

Of passionate caresses.

The touch of his hand
A thousand lotuses
Drawing her closer
Her sweetness and beauty
Resembles pink roses.

Into his heart
He touches her soul
Energy magnetism
Never to be controlled.

Her eyes as blue as the deep blue sea
His eyes like raw cacao of sweet ecstasy
The sweet allure of his sweat and warm face
Where time stands still
Suspended in bliss – tender embrace.

The whole world could end
Caught up in their bliss
The sexy allure
Of their first kiss.

WILDFLOWER

The only witness high up above

Her mystical seduction

Of the Lunar night sky

The moment passed

The saltiness remains

The masculine divine

Sweat sublime of infinity

Lingers upon her beautiful lips

A new day dawns

For she is the goddess of the moon

Her body a temple of delights

Of mystical sensuality

Curvaceous and strong

A roaring vulnerability.

Set free with unlimited passion

She's fearless and awakened

Of new possibility

Exploring and learning

Unlimited imagination
And creativity
Downloads are flowing
Like a raging river.

Her body vibrating
Her heart of infinity
There is no slowing
The Goddess of the moon.
Try to control her
You will lose her too soon.

Like a passing storm
She will be gone,
Free will and passion
Exploring her sensuality
Of creative expression.

Pure passion expanded
Feminine flow of divinity

WILDFLOWER

All humanity entwined

Unified in love – cosmic life force.

Soul truth of love & oneness

Only remains

There is no room for hate

Or jealousy,

Clear up your bullshit and

Your rules of blind expectation.

Enjoy your dance

Of deep sensuality

Sweet simplicity of romance

Be free to dance

Of your own free will.

Meet others with truth

Love & compassion

Express your spirit & passion

Awakened within.

Chapter 9: Expressing Intimate Desires

> *"Words are seeds that do more than blow around. They land in your heart and not the ground. Be careful what you plant and careful what you say. You might have to eat what you have planted one day".*
>
> - Unknown

Choosing your Vibe

The universe does not choose if it is good or bad, it will deliver the most consistent and under-lying resonance to assist your growth. It takes a high level of personal responsibility to choose your thoughts wisely, and it is vital to shift direction when and as needed. It all comes back to you. It can be confronting to find yourself in a place that you don't like, simply because as another has chosen a path that suits their needs and desires better. No matter which way you look at it, always rewind to the initial interaction of intention and take responsibility for your actions.

What was your intention when you first met? Did you see them as an equal being or did you see a way to weave them into your game/agenda? This is manipulation when you remove the masks of the story.

For example: did you fear them mistrusting you? This fear will attract what you are putting out, meaning this is what you will see in every area of your life. They may be stepping away as they have their own vision and dream. Life will bring you exactly what you need to grow from. Rewind back to the *re-claiming your womb power* and have compassion for all by trusting in letting go of the past and break free from any contracts that no longer serve You.

She is unapologetic by design and free

A picture of me in my 40's, embracing the sacred feminine as art, unapologetic, shameless and owning my natural embodiment of light wild in nature. The photographer is Tim Bradshaw for his Exhibition with 40 + Nude Models.

DIFFERENT STATES ON THE ENERGY RESONANCE SCALE.

High Vibration:

Love- Peace- Presence- Harmony- Happiness- Joy- Truth- Free expression - Compassion– Honesty- Rapture- Sharing- Caring- Stillness- Unity- Oneness.

All are high vibe emotions and actions create constructive motion.

Low Vibration:

Consistent anger- Mistrust- Un-forgiveness- Shame- Blame- Jealousy- Self-doubt- Guilt- Judgment of self and others- Hate- Disgust- Being mean- Ruminating- Lying and Speaking badly of others.

Anger is a healthy when released, expressed with no harm to Self or others. Anger that is unexpressed can manifest as a state of depression!

All states of resonance will attract more things that reflect the exact underlying emotion. With patience and a willingness to accept change each emotion has an opportunity to evolve. *Sadness* is a necessary emotion to allow the grieving and letting go so never push it away, I invite you to be courageous and stay with it. Each emotion has a contrast and super happiness is the contrast to sadness. Have the courage to transcend the sadness by giving it space to be expressed, accepted and honoured. Your emotions can feel wild and deep and are your connection to Spirit. Each is thus a powerful messenger to reveal the truth of what is happening beneath your skin. This is why addressing the mind and your thoughts is key to create the right actions to live a life of freedom and freedom from suffering.

It is beautiful to speak the unspoken and express within a kiss of natural flowing energy that builds and creates an intoxicating allure of one another's energy and breath. A dance where both are breathing and feeling into the pulse of one resonance of auric fields blending. A perfect interlude to wet your lips before we explore expressing with raw vulnerability.

> *'Poetry is freedom to express what your heart may be scared to reveal in spoken words'*
>
> Zoe Bell

<u>Bliss of the kiss</u>

A delicious kiss,

A magnetic pull,

Between lips is fierce.

Lips slightly brushing

Two breathes dancing,

Spirits exploring.

Souls intertwining,

Bodies tingling

Senses awakening,

The sacred allure and timing

Of the first kiss.

UP LEVEL YOUR RELATIONSHIP

Let's explore ways to deepen intimacy, build connection and shift from where maybe you are at. This is an invitation to provide some guidance to get to where you wish to be. This relates to all relationships, both business and personal. Modify the questions to be relevant with each environment. Every interaction with a soul is intimate when one is communicating from the heart with unconditional love. To build trust, faith whilst stepping forward with courage, begins with self and realization of the 'I'. Yes, you have to be the change and create the life you want and stop waiting for others to make the first move.

EXPRESS RAW VULNERABILITY

As you realise that the power of your consistent thoughts, words, emotions and actions have a direct relationship to what happens in life, you begin to open up a deeper understanding. This is life-changing and a wake up for many. Address this with courage, personal commitment and focus. Even if your words, desires are not met with the response you want, be brave to express it. The universe is always listening especially when you say what you want and a knowing of what you deserve. A deep and passionate heartfelt desire is heard far beyond and even in your darkest sorrow the universe is lining up another Soul that is far more suited to your life. By being stuck in fear of rejection, you may stop those words of your raw heart from coming out and hiding behind fear; learn to let go of any agenda, have a clear intention and express your truth in direct and loving communication. Expressing your vulnerable heart is the scariest and most magical action you can do in life as what awaits on the other side of fear by expressing your truth, is love. Raw vulnerability is very different to staying a victim of your circumstances and allowing external forces to manipulate your vulnerability into a society of control. Using your vulnerability to hook and manipulate others is a clever game of victim consciousness. Be willing to stand up for what is right and do better and live with integrity.

Deepen Intimacy

Emotional connection creates trust in self and the courage to express and honour the messages revealing. Listening with presence is vital and to be aware of inner judgment as it arises. To truly know-thy-self is to let go, meaning to be free of attachment to outcomes and any expectation of the other. This is a peaceful womb warrior's path towards self-mastery, and you simply have to connect to the Feminine Source Spirit within.

Communicate your heartfelt desires.

- Be present in your listening
- Connect to their mind before their body
- IN-TO-ME-SEE - See the reflection or the mirror of truth
- Listen to his or her heart
- Hear one another's words
- Maintain soft eye contact
- Listen to what is not been said in the space

- Be open and hear the other person's emotions and words
- Let all judgment of fantasies go and all expectations
- Know and express openly your energetic boundaries
- Be flexible and open to explore
- Be in a space of emotional intelligence and be discerning in all words expressed.

CREATE TRUST

Trust assists in feeling safe to acknowledge your feelings and the courage to express them. It may be the courage of one to fully open their heart and to fall forwards in faith. To trust that no matter the outcome all will align for the best. Be willing to trust one another and resist the urge to manipulate, convince or control one other. Unless you can learn to trust again then there is no moving forward. You either choose to trust your partner and self or you choose to step away and allow one another the space to move on with your lives. Never bring up old stuff from the past, it's not fair and will attract more of that specific drama. Once the lesson is learnt and insight gained then the past has zero business in the NOW. This requires letting go, holding space in compassion and allowing forgiveness. Either move forwards together in alignment or walk separate ways on your own paths. A relationship without trust is shaky in its foundations and will eventually crack. This is how codependency in relationships plays out, both afraid to step away as they have become dependable on one another. Trust requires regaining through intentions and actions and this will take as long as it needs for each individual. Remember to see the best in your partner as life is never black and white! Life is many shades of grey with splashes of colour and when the colour in the relationship disappears, it is calling for a revamp or it is dead. There are no sides in relationships, it all comes back to self. Those that find it hard to trust others, simply, do not trust themselves! You learn and grow through relationships as an imperfect human.

Set Boundaries

Boundaries are what you will and will not accept, the *'line in the sand'*. Boundaries with intentions require setting at the beginning of any relationship, as together they create a safe container with stable foundations. Be mindful of rules and ultimatums as these are based on lack and fear. Something to keep in mind; the less rules for your partner to jump through the simpler the relationship will be. Honesty is vital and the willingness to hear your partner with love. Boundaries are energetic, physical, spiritual and psychological, as all energy exchange is sacred. Life is a sensual field of wonder and sacred energy boundaries are a message of self-love, self-worth and how you are choosing to show up in life.

Know your Boundaries

This may be explored at the beginning of a relationship where both are learning through trial and error. Boundaries show up where there is moment to moment presence. If you share an experience and it wasn't really what you like of enjoy then express your insights within a sacred space with your partner. Be willing to be brave and honest, without blaming or making it about them. If you are attempting to convince the another or what you are trying to say by using many words, then it can escalate into a chaotic mess. This is an ego of rightness and arrogance feeling uncomfortable by not feeling the inner needs have been met and projecting onto the other. Relationships grow and evolve by exploring your tastes together and apart. Before you enter any situation with other parties make sure you both have safe boundaries and make sure that you make eyes contact with their eyes, especially if this is around sensual exploration. Be willing to show them everything, your fantasies, your tastes and your kinks. It is best to communicate these and play it out in a fantasy with the two of you first. Remember your pleasure is his or her pleasure and vice versa. There is no making one right and the other wrong or pointing the finger of what is good or bad, that is a conversation with your own conscience. Relationship is about meeting in the middle. This requires trust and a deep love for one another. Inviting others into your pleasure is not for everyone, you can keep exploring in fantasy until you are both ready, it has to be a mutual agreement and in no way threatens you on a deep level. The boundaries can and may change in the moment, so be willing to be flexible to all needs and never use boundaries as a punishment and withholding out of spite; it may create a nasty backfire. Respect a no and stop when a no is heard. Always be there for the one you love; you are the core and the solid foundation. You may find that as souls you may grow apart, and that he or she is no longer aligned with your life path. Be willing to honour all messages as it is your heart and soul speaking to you.

'Boundaries are self-love and until every soul commits to self-mastery as a top priority then boundaries are vital. Oneness has become superficial, and sensuality is losing its sacred purity with the more you invite into the broth'. Zoe Bell

The inward path to dissolving identification of self, the masks, labels require working towards zero attachment. This takes a lot of deep inner soul work and the courage to keep letting go of what you think you know and letting go of the love that you may find yourselves being consumed by. Many have been choosing a path of abstinence and letting go of any desire to perform. This may show up as observing the patterns of behaviour like shaving your legs, waxing your bush, all as a performance for acceptance and to look sexy. The patterns are so ingrained into society and when you start to look at why you do things, many times it is to get something outside of self, or an expectation of a social condition. This time of seclusion and being in integrity with self is a vital step in preparation for sacred sensuality with a soul that is also holding self in the highest level of sovereignty and is fully invested in the deep inner work. A path that presents to be devoted to a path of service of Source as a vessel for divine light of pure love to flow through.

As You each become more crystalline in structure meaning less dense the physical form will disappear altogether. You as a being will be able to walk into one another's energetic fields as a choice of energy exchange or a transfer and upgrade DNA. Each time You do this, I feel it will be like having an orgasmic experience and as these higher vibrational light beings, you may have up to 10 or more orgasms a day. I am currently exploring with a 7D being from the Pleiades, my home and he is guiding me in the teachings of sacred sensuality as our Spirit bodies weave, intertwine and each moment feels whole body orgasmic. I feel peace, pure love and I am in full choice of all I am exploring. As we each evolve boundaries will become obsolete as all communication shifts into telepathic with transparency of all thought form waves. This is an exciting for humanity as there is huge quantum leap over the next 9-years, till 2030. I have witnessed in dreams bodies combusting by bursting into flames as they have not done the inner work to upgrade the bodysuit. As the higher frequency came in their bodysuits were unable to hold the vibration. Dreams reveal much and

I often have a prescience, a knowing before an event. Who knows if this will happen?

OPEN COMMUNICATION

Enquire, listen and feel and be in presents space for open communication. Openness requires being judgment-free with the flexibility to be fluid to change, moment to moment. When any emotion arises, sit with it and explore the deeper meaning, and then be in choice if it requires expressing, or be still and silent. Gain the insight and when ready allow it to pass through or express from a place of love. All that arises is an opportunity to learn and grow into adulthood. A partner that loves you will listen and hear your voice whilst holding the door open and at times stand on the edge with you, until you are read to leap, pause or step away. You each have the freedom to choose your unique direction. Keep all communication open with one another as there is nothing to hide. Never be afraid to express when your needs are not being met as everyone has a different sensual need in the way they like being touched, honoured or their language of love.

Perhaps, there is a way to meet in the middle, so all needs are heard and met, or perhaps have outgrown one another. It is a beautiful experience when the doors of communication are open, and all communication is met with love, respect, honesty and trust.

BE IN NON-JUDGMENT

Play can be used to bring lightness if your partner is more sexually experienced than You. Allow him or her to lead and walk alongside you as doors of experience are opened and see each experience with curiosity as the first time. Never ask, *how many people have you slept with?* This is childish and is a digging into the past to use as ammunition, often called baiting caused by insecurity. It has zero relevance to the person in the present moment and can open up a can of worms. Never ask the question if you are unable to hear and handle the truth and address the inner reactions of judgment. What You have experienced, explored or chosen in the past in no one else's business, period. If you wish to share, then do so with light curiosity and innocent wonder. Be grateful as now you are with this divine Soul that you love and has a colourful sensual experience to share with you. You too will have had good teachers from your past and not everything requires a postmortem.

Answer all questions with as little self-judgment or protected judgement in the best way you can. Remember you have attracted the relationship for what you are here to learn to love, embrace and let go of. Be brave to be the version you are stepping into as a sexy, sassy and classy flower. This does not mean bulldozing others with your words that lash out as you are unable to receive.

My intention was to bring awareness into how porn is highly destructive for evolving sacred sensuality. Porn is manipulative and a low vibration that sucks the soul dry, feeding on lust, guilt and shame. It is blocking the mind from its own wild and creative imagination. The right-side of the brain, the creative imagination is desiring to be nourished, and the subconscious marinated and stirred, and porn is tapping into the dopamine rush and creates harmful addictions. This is explored in deeper depths in *Soul Codes*.

Intimacy

Your words unspoken

Tickle my soul

Depths unspoken

Whispered in my dream

To dance within your soul

Depths of burning passion

A river runs deep

Awakening a deep sleep

We meet and swim

In an ocean of bliss

Fearless abandonment

Deeper into our Abyss

The warmth of your body

As drawn me in close.

My heart skips a beat

As I meet your embrace

The truth that you speak

Rips straight into my heart

WILDFLOWER

Words of such depth and passion

Can never keep us apart

A language of love all new to me

An unspoken romance

Grows within

Only imagined in my dreams.

I have to be candid

A masculine man expressing his truth

My language of deep love,

Passion and words that excite me

A willingness to dive in deep

Into the unknown

Courageous- carefree

To dance on our own

Love secrets mystery.

I feel the warmth of your words playing in my heart

A depth of spirits never held apart

A life force connection runs a course of its own

EXPRESSING INTIMATE DESIRES

Free will and adventure

What is this adventure?

We explore as one

As I feel you close

Together as One.

Your words of truth have awakened my heart

A secret key to unlocking my truth

A gift to now share with humanity

Till death us do part

To have been left broken

To never fall apart

All part of this journey

To heal my heart

To fear no disappointment

To be in this moment

Enjoying the dance

Sweet evolving love romance

The anticipation of your lips

WILDFLOWER

The invitation of tenderness

A sweet ecstasy brewing

A smile that awakens

New possibility

To dive in deeper

The most beautiful journey

A sweet love of self

IN-TO-ME-SEE

CONCLUSION

> *"If you want to win hearts, sow the seeds of love. If you want heaven, stop scattering thorns on the road."* - Rumi

How are you feeling beautiful Soul? Take a moment to pause with a deep breath and see what arises in the silence.

I am curious; do you feel more connected into your natural sensual essence? Perhaps, questions have arisen, or some confusion mixed in with excitement. Is your soul infused with rich inspiration excited to explore more about yourself and intimate relationships?

Are you feeling an awakening within your wild flowering Yoni as your star blossoming awakens? As a man, are you gaining a deeper insight into the wisdom of the feminine woman and the holy sacredness of the divine feminine goddess within? No matter your biology as Star seeds you are blossoming.

I am a totally different to when I first released my story in 2015 and the journey of sacred sensuality is ever evolving. Each moment, I feel my soul unravelling into the sweetest nectar of simplicity whilst restoring purity beyond the over-sexualised programing bound in society.

Holy f*ck, to gaze back to the raw innocence of finding my way through the dark jungle of a chaotic mess as the initial story began to flow out of me, is beautiful to witness. The raw sensual exploration reads almost pornographic and yet what I was expressing was my fearless innocence and I held nothing back. I was standing for sensual empowerment in my raw flesh and yet my vessel was lusted over by men and women. I say this to invite you to be willing to keep getting messy and to express within each moment. Don't waste your life by sitting on the fence as the spectator afraid of what others will say. Be brave to fall and explore the game of life as only then do you truly begin to understand the meaning of living. Even from January 2020 to now, August 2021 are quantum leaps in creative expression and the way I show up in feminine softness, which is innocence wrapped into a deep inner knowing.

> *'In those moments of insanity, I tasted the riches of an infinite ocean of love where I bathed drunk on bliss'*
> Zoe Anna Bell

CONCLUSION

I am from Pleiades here in embodied human form...

I am an awakening of sensuality and raw source creativity as a doorway to invite you to leap into the unknown and go deeper within. I know this without a shadow of a doubt that who you were at the beginning of the book to who you are now is an ignited remembrance of your sensual freedom and radiant inner glow. Be badass with your feminine power in full flowering radiance. This picture created by my beautiful Pleiadian Sistar, Sarah Polyakov.

In the space between your words, I hear your Soul – Zoe

I am wondering what the response will be, the look on your face, the contours of your mouth as you read the content, and a raw navigation.

Perhaps, longing moments of biting your bottom lip as you get to taste the nectar within You. I have no attachment to this either, as it is time to set this free. This is your journey of loving implementation with tender introspection. To remember the adventure and yet, fragility of life.

> *Her lifetime She leapt to realise she leapt alone and there reveals how she learnt to fly alone until another grew wings* – Zoe

I am sure you will have gained a deeper understanding into the relationship with your sacred womb wisdom, body resonance and ways to heal your life. We the wise women are supporting one another to raise consciousness to restore innocence lost, hidden and forgotten and to hold the line so men grow into adulthood. A path of pure sensuality, freedom of choice and to be unapologetically wild as You. There is no competition as there is room for all to blossom and there is no urgency, we complement one another.

> *Her poetic words weave your heart strings gently tugging a deeper arousal of your spirits inner calling* – Zoe

I look forward to sharing with you, *Soul Codes- Remembering your Mission*. All relevant keys to evolve as a magnetic soul and vital teachings for team humanity. These are steppingstones to navigate the raging rivers and infinite ocean of life with your eternal flame of passion guiding the way.

CONCLUSION

May this book be a fresh opening of your heart, leaving your soul challenged and dripping in rich inspiration. Each inner reaction and external response are divinely orchestrated to remember your greatest badass-beautiful Self. See the reflective diamond of You and continue this infinite self-exploration of your magical inner garden of heaven on Earth within. Each reaction is a signpost to be curious to explore beyond the fear, the doubt or gnawing inner pain you have ignored for way too long. Wake-up from the deep sleep of your sensual repression and get excited with confusion, overwhelm and the despair moments as they are signposts for growth. All is never lost as you have to lose self to reveal a deeper expression, ready to re-birth. A path of intimacy begins with each individual taking self-responsibility, initiations to test integrity, owning your no, as when you say yes to life, life synchronises pathways to follow. Remember, life is an invitation to meet your highest self, continue to undress the unknown and open the eyes of your lovers in this life. Follow your gut, your instinct, question everything and your hearts fearless bliss.

You have the power to be, do and have anything you chose as You are learning, growing and expanding moment to moment.

> *'I am ready to expand beyond anything I have ever known; I am ready as I am limitless. I am on a mission to assist in healing humanity with tidal waves of love in healing the rage and misconception around intimacy and sensuality. It is your light and your human right to embody this cosmic bliss.'* – Zoe

It is time to embrace the deeper aspects of your inner sparkle, explore the practices to awaken your light-body and with awareness, access higher levels of orgasmic bliss and integration all to activate your divine Soul Codes of your mission. May this be a key towards getting crystal clear on your Soul remembrance and mission for humanity. I love you infinitely in all your raw and messy jaggedness. Embrace each perceived flaw as a unique thread guiding you home as you are all fractals within this colourful tapestry called life.

2020 was an attempt of a Great Awakening of the masses to rinse out and purify what had been hidden within the shadows for so long. Ascension began to be known for many more, from many more waking up for 2018 as the veil of consciousness thinned. I see 2021 and beyond of guiding many, a time for massive leaps in upgrades, DNA acceleration and transformation from 3rd dimensional consciousness and into the sacred heart known as 4th dimensional consciousness whilst remaining embodied in the physical.

Together and united, those born from the late 1960's to the early 1980's, are the second wave of inspiration that humanity cried called out. If you are drawn to my work, then you and I are soul family as these dates are simply a range and not set in stone. And so, it is, and so it is and so it is…

To bring this into some form of completion I am opening up an invitation for you to know thy self and remember who you are, and for the men to remember the feminine source power within you.

CONCLUSION

Be free to express beyond social conditioning. Sensuality is learnt through direct experiences of expanding the edges to refine your hearts vocabulary – Zoe Anna

A WOMAN OF EASE & GRACE

A woman of ease and grace radiates electromagnetic energy and a glowing light as her auric rainbow essence. Her feminine softness radiates easeful magnetic flow that requires zero force. Her presence is felt by others as an embodiment of the sacred masculine and divine feminine, that have aligned into a Sacred divine Union. She is unafraid to allow raw passion and un-wavering sharp focus to be expressed in her fearless action. There is a lightness of ease, and tender surrender within her vulnerability. She dances between playfulness, creativity and poetic expression by challenging the edges of conformity. She thrives with Soul freedom and seeks to explore beyond. She cares little for societal rules of conformity within the rigid rightness-wrongness of opinion, as she has broken free of the illusion of entrapment. She has the ability to process the energy that she absorbs, clearing karmic threads and her eyes penetrate deep into your heart and soul. Are you recognizing her yet? Feel your way in by allowing these words to drip open your soul. She is sensual healing essence in manifested form and her spirit weaves the dance. Do not confuse this purity with a seductress that manipulates with her unhealed sexual power!

Her poetic words weave within around your heart strings gently tugging a deeper arousal of your free spirits inner calling – Zoe Bell

The path of feminine rising takes courage with much time in solitude and discernment in how to work with the sensual healing energy. This path requires unapologetic, deep inner healing and de-programming the sexual games of the slut programming and sexual seductress. The ego will hide this and will resist letting it go as it will not want to admit it, as it slithers in the darkness of lust and denial.

This inner work is cleansing and purifying of innocence lost, and she may find it is the nature spirits that counsel her cries and where she seeks guidance the most. Guidance is delivered in her dream state, and she trusts in the message's moment to moment. This woman does not seek it outside herself.

She is fearless to step away, as she honours her boundaries, and will endeavor to gaze at all with compassion, loving kindness, always beginning with Self. She is raw and real and has fallen flat on her face more times than being rewarded or seen. She continues to dance within the flames with fearless passions as her wild free spirit is here to explore and lead others. She is sovereign and has spent many years re-storing the sacredness of her womb temple back into pure innocence of light. She has been tested, rejected and abandoned and she has learnt to never reject her soul mission for humanity. Her passion is overwhelming and intoxicating as she is following a feeling larger than life. She has risen above lustful desires felt by men and women as she called back her womb wisdom and the layers of healing shame held bound from her past story of pain and sexual slut programming. Many have tasted her nectar of life as she mirrored back their own inner darkness. A sacred space where they too began to face their greatest fears and ventured upon the walk alone, until they too learnt how to unfu*k themselves from the lower frequencies.

CONCLUSION

She has the strength of an elephant and holds the whole world in her sacred heart, a divine sweet nectar of soma, the most potent elixir that flows like honey pulsating through her veins and dancing with every cell of her being.

This sacred woman carries the Holy Sophia Codes and Rose Lineage of Womb wisdom, and she is within each and all of You!

Her path requires diligence as many women are curious of her yet feel threatened as many men will desire her. This desire shifts into shamming her and judging her wild spirit. This is how the sacred feminine within you all was suppressed and manipulated by patriarchal society and the birthing of the masculine consciousness. This woman feels it all and her mission is to open doors to lead the way and be a bridge to assist this quantum leap in all sensuality, healing humanity and into the feminine consciousness of the new Earth. The new Earth is not outside of You, it is the enchanted forest within you. She is a healer, dancer, white witch, shaman and guide that seeks the truth. She has stood alone and away from the crowd; Often seen dancing around the circles of sisters, never feeling she belonged. She was welcomed to sit with the brothers, that for many years were her protectors. Her initiation is now complete, and she holds scared space for both the brothers and the sisters as we are all One.

Each day, she navigates new layers, releases tension from her meat body suit, so she can breathe into each sensual moment. Life is sensual, her entire expression is sensual as she is cosmic light and bliss. Her heart is calling out for a sacred man that will mirror her devotion to serve humanity and to reach higher states of cosmic bliss where two divine unions merge. She is patient as she trusts in divine timing.

WILDFLOWER

You will find her dancing within the flames, joyful and content and savouring the sweet offerings of life that nature presents in joyous abundance. Thank you for sharing this journey with me and diving into the sacredness of the womb wisdom and a topic close to my heart, the flowering and sacred yoni.

Magnetic orgasmic pulses of Cosmic pure love,

May you enjoy the opening of the Yoni-verse!

Wildflower's healing and Wild Spirits remembering

Star seeds blossoming

BIBLIOGRAPHICAL RESOURCES

We each have a powerful mission. Allow the books to choose you, as we each have different paths to follow and express freely. Allow books to choose you and your intuitive wisdom guiding you.

Reclaiming Goddess Sexuality - The Power of the Feminine Way (1999),

By Linda. E. Savage

"The Science of" trilogy, by Wallace D. Wattles

– The Science of Getting Rich (1910)

– The Science of Being Great (1910)

– The Science of Being Well (1910)

The Master Key System (1912), by Charles F. Haanel

Absolute Happiness (1993), by Michael Domeyko Rowland

Experiences in life as Becky Bell and Zoe Bell /Zoe Anna

Acknowledgments

To my wildflower in her unapologetic design in full bloom thank you for guiding me where to heal and a vital aspect of the path I was here to guide others. What I shamed and rejected was my medicine.

All those who took without asking and taught me to ignite my inner roaring fire to stand up for my rites. To those who attempted to shame me with derogatory names, thank you.

To all those that have thrown stones, talked behind my back, thank you as I learnt to walk alone and allow the skin to become flexible to change and learn to fall in love deeply with self. You each were wise teachers in this path of empowerment to love the aspects I was still rejecting.

To the Artist of the Womb Art cover Emma Plunkett, a brilliant artist from the UK and living in Barcelona. A strong woman that stands for Feminine rights and free expression of sensuality. Thank you for your brilliant service towards sensuality and the Power of the Womb and feminine Voice.

To you the reader, for being drawn to my work to empower both men, women and youth. May this be a cornerstone to your own self-discovery to fall in love with the aspects you have shamed or compared your uniqueness to others.

To my beloved seer- sistars and seer-brothers that truly see me and my two children that have witnessed this coming into creation and birth. I know at times you would have preferred that I write cookbooks and hey, this is who I am.

May this be a recipe to inner stand women and sensuality as you explore the sweet tasting of love in all your relationships. You are gifts, two beautiful souls and this is part of my soul path. I love you Jake and Charlie unconditionally. Endeavor to live each day unapologetically and shamelessly. Even if no one else understands your path, have the courage to follow it through as you each follow your courageous hearts.

To my soul, thank you for never giving up on me.

ABOUT THE AUTHOR

Zoe Anna Bell – A Relationship Guide, international Healer, Shaman, Published Author and assisting healing Trauma in womb healing.

She is leading a way in Sacred Sensuality and Conscious relating whilst empowering women to own their voices.

She lives in Sydney, with her two teenage boys and spends her days writing poetry and holding space for healing the mind-body. A leader of the New Earth.

She runs international retreats, workshops and is available for speaking engagements.

www.zoe-anna.com

Sales Page

Looking to stay connected? I would love to support you through your journey and welcome your feedback.

Trilogy Book Series

Breaking FREE – No more Soul Suffocation

WILDFLOWER – Reclaiming a Sacred Place

Soul CODES – Remembering your Mission

Other books:

RAW- The Key to a Woman's Heart & Soul.

COMPLETENESS- A Doorway to Love

Healing Prolapse – Shannon Dunn

(Co-authored a chapter on the divine feminine & sacred masculine)

https://www.linkedin.com/in/zoe-anna-bell/

https://instagram.com/zoeanna_bell/

www.zoe-anna.com / info@zoe-anna.com

www.ingramcontent.com/pod-product-compliance
Lightning Source LLC
Chambersburg PA
CBHW050310010526
44107CB00055B/2177